AROUND THE WORLD
IN A
CEMENT BOAT

The *Berenice* sailing somewhere off the coast of Africa in 1973.
Dad steers at the tiller. David, a crewman, sits on the stern railing
near the dinghy. Mom sits in the cockpit. Cheryl's blonde head
peeks out of the doorway of the main cabin.

AROUND THE WORLD
IN A
CEMENT BOAT

A Young Girl's True Adventure

CHERYL TRZASKO

iUniverse, Inc.
Bloomington

Around the World in a Cement Boat
A Young Girl's True Adventure

iUniverse books may be ordered through booksellers or by contacting:

iUniverse
1663 Liberty Drive
Bloomington, IN 47403
www.iuniverse.com
1-800-Authors (1-800-288-4677)

ISBN: 978-1-4759-7558-1 (sc)
ISBN: 978-1-4759-7559-8 (ebk)

Library of Congress Control Number: 2013902419

Printed in the United States of America

iUniverse rev. date: 02/08/2013

To my dear husband and all the little ones we've loved,
whether ours forever or just temporarily,
and
To the Master of All Creation who brought me safely to this point

Psalm 107:23-31

TABLE OF CONTENTS

1. THE CYCLONE

Sep. 21, 1971

Crunched into a corner of the bunk, my bare toes pushed against the lip of the wooden berth. My heels dug into the vinyl cushion. Every muscle tense, I fought to stay put. I felt like I'd been here, in this position, forever.

By my side, Jolene clung on, too. Together, my five-year-old little sister and I struggled simply to stay in one place. That doesn't sound so hard; does it? But we'd fought this battle, on and off, for an eternity. Okay, it had only been a few days, but even a couple of minutes of this felt like forever.

I'd lost track of Pierre-Paul, the four-year-old son of two of our crew. Maybe I should call him "the terror of the ship" instead. In the gloom, I couldn't see much in the galley, but he must still be in his bunk in the bow where he'd retreated a while ago. He'd be safe enough there, not that I worried much about him, given all that he'd done. Well, I didn't wholly blame him. His parents were the real problem. Still, I was glad I didn't have to look out for him, too, right now.

I was only six-and-a-half years old, but as the oldest child onboard, I took on the job of watching the other kids. Well, Mom took care of Jackie, my three-and-a-half month old baby sister, but I kept Jolene and Pierre-Paul out of the way of the busy grownups as much as possible. A lot of grown-ups said I acted too mature for my age, but Mom told me she appreciated the assistance. Besides, I wasn't allowed to work with the crew sailing the ship, and I wanted to help somehow.

At first, I'd entertained five-year-old Jolene and four-year-old Pierre-Paul with stories, but the storm became too much. Like a toddler having a tantrum, screaming and tossing a rag doll this way and that, ripping it apart in anger, the cyclone flung us about. School lessons and toys were forgotten. Holding on became all we thought about. Damp, miserable, and scared, we worked to survive.

The *Berenice* lurched again, and I slammed against the bulkhead between the galley and the head. The leeboard, the canvas curtain strung across the front of the bunk and tucked under the mattress, helped prevent us from flying to the floor below. I clutched the rope strung through the leeboard, bracing myself. I didn't want to slam against the wall, again, when the next lurch came.

At times, the ship jerked rapidly from side to side and bucked like a wild horse. Other times, it rolled this way and that, before building up to a series of fierce slams. Through it all, we hung on as best we could.

I shifted my bent knees and repositioned my hands, clutching the rope again. Beside me, I felt Jolene rub her head before she grabbed on again, too.

"You okay?" I yelled, but Jolene didn't say a word. Of course she didn't. Who could hear anything over the racket that had filled our ears for days? Roaring winds, pounding waves, driving sheets of rain blocked out all other sound. Or maybe she did say something which I couldn't hear.

Hours later, sunlight peeked through the heavy clouds, bringing a little daylight into the cabin. Rubbing my eyes, I looked around. Inside the cabin, everything was damp and musty smelling. Water dripped through the slats of the cabin door. Since everything had been strapped down or stored away days ago, the cabin was remarkably tidy despite the wild ride.

Through the portholes, I gazed out at the waves. Really, I should say "wave," because there was only one wave. A wave so huge, I couldn't see its top or sides. Up and up it went, like a skyscraper. If such a monstrous wall of water collapsed on us . . . Well, imagine dumping a barrelful of water onto a paper cup floating in a bathtub; the cup would be smashed to the bottom immediately. That's why the adults scurried about so much, leaving me to take care of my little sister and myself.

The motion of *Berenice* calmed enough that we could sit without a fight. As though a giant hand had turned down the volume of the wind and waves, other sounds emerged. Rrrip. Crack! A sail split as the spinnaker pole supporting it broke under the strain of another gust of wind. Dad yelled something from his post at the wheel. Footsteps pounded as Claude, a New Zealander, and his French wife, Marie, raced to save the spinnaker's remnants. Claude and Marie were the crewmembers who knew nothing about disciplining brats.

In the galley, utensils clattered against the pans on the stove as Mom finished cooking lunch. The stove swung wildly front to back and side to side, but the double set of hinged brackets did their job, keeping the stove horizontal despite the movement of the yacht. Pots and pans stayed in place even when people couldn't.

"Lunchtime. Come and get it!" yelled Mom, a pretty, curly-haired American in her late twenties. She grabbed a bowl from the shelf where a series of bars held dishes secure. She spooned in some vegetable stew, and then added a hunk of damper. The Australian pan bread and stew should have smelled delicious, but the wet-dog smell of the cabin and the bile in my throat blotted out other scents.

Dark-haired, slender Pierre-Paul scampered in from the front bedroom. He grabbed the bowl, spoon, and cup of water that Mom offered. Then he plopped down on the berth opposite us.

"Wait for grace," Mom reminded him, and he lowered his spoon with a grunt.

"Come on, girls," she said, holding out another bowl.

"I don't feel like eating," I protested, clutching my roiling stomach. Though I had my sea legs, my tummy couldn't handle this wild motion.

"Cheryl, you need to eat. Everyone needs to eat. It'll keep us going," she insisted, with a smile.

Reluctantly, I got up and took the bowl she offered.

Strawberry-blonde, freckled Jolene sighed. Then she plodded over and took her food, too. Sitting down, she looked at it warily. Jolene was never seasick, but the extreme weather took a toll even on her stomach.

"How you manage to make meals during this kind of weather, I'll never know," Bill said, shaking his head, as he plopped down at the table beside Pierre-Paul. Bill was an Australian bloke who'd joined our crew along with Pierre-Paul's family.

Mom smiled uneasily at him. She suspected him of stirring up trouble behind the scenes and didn't trust his silver tongue, but she tried to be polite.

With a squeal, the hatch in the ceiling slid back, and the door underneath banged opened. Pounding rain hurtled in, swirling through the cabin with a howling wind, making each of us shiver. A figure in bright yellow foul-weather gear hustled down the companionway ladder, latching the door and slamming the hatch closed. The yellow rain hood slid back to reveal a dripping wet Marie.

After Marie's dash to the head (or bathroom, as I used to call it in my landlubber days), Mom said the blessing and the meal began.

Marie snatched the mug of hot coffee Mom offered and held it close to her unnaturally red face. Closing her eyes, she inhaled the steam and warmed her hands around the cup before taking a sip. Dripping wet, she stood, rather than soak the berths. Not that it made much difference, since everything onboard was damp from days of storm.

Each of us held our plate, cup, and utensils, rather than allow the cyclone to dump them off the table. I drank a sip or two so there'd be less liquid to slosh out, and then I clutched the cup with my thighs. Holding my bowl and fork in one hand and the damper in the other, I stared at the bread for a while, but I couldn't bring myself to take a bite. The thought of another swallow sent my stomach into spasms.

"Eat. Eat. You never eat." Marie said to Pierre-Paul, out of habit. She always worried that he wouldn't eat, which seemed silly since he ate whatever Mom served. Then again, Marie cooked for us once, but mutiny seemed likely if she ever tried that again.

No one had the heart for chitchat. Each stared silently at the food, lost in thought, listening to the sounds of the storm outside and the clinking of spoons against bowls inside.

As the meal ended, Pierre-Paul demanded, "Juice, Mommy, Juice."

Marie dropped her spoon into her bowl, and hustled to get her son some more water. In his vocabulary, "juice" meant a drink.

No one asked for seconds. I hadn't even tasted my original serving. Mom shook her head as I handed her my plate, but she took it without a word, and I sat again, clutching my stomach. She put my food away for the next meal, since we couldn't afford to waste anything.

A lurch of the hull and new noises from outside brought my thoughts back to the galley. Marie handed her dishes to Mom, pulled up her rain hood, and scurried back up the ladder to the cockpit, back into the cyclone.

Her husband, Claude, came down minutes later, bringing the storm back into the cabin for a moment. He took his turn eating lunch, but Dad wouldn't come down. For days, he'd refused to leave the helm, except for bathroom breaks, so Mom donned a set of foul-weather gear and took the meal to him instead. When she returned, she cleaned the remaining dishes, and fixed Jackie a bottle of formula.

Baby Jackie was the youngest of the nine people aboard our 39-foot yacht. Believe it or not, she seemed to enjoy this nightmare. Wrapped snugly, warm in her basket which was wedged securely in the v-shaped area between the two forward bunks, she slept pretty much around the clock, lulled to sleep by the cacophony of the storm and the rattling chains in the sail locker behind the bulkhead, and rocked by the unpredictable motion of the boat.

Soon enough, the respite ended. The rays of sunlight disappeared. Voices and other sounds faded away as the roar of the wind and sea grew loud enough to hurt my ears. The motion of the ship grew violent and unpredictable again. Jolene and I were back on the berth, in the dark, holding on for dear life.

After Mom served another meal that I couldn't eat, I managed to sleep, right there on my upper berth in the galley. Jolene dozed on the lower berth in front of mine. How we managed to stay put, I'm not sure. The leeboard helped, but I suspect our muscles kept doing the jobs they'd memorized. Maybe we didn't sleep well, but we could doze off during the day. The adults didn't have that choice. Around the clock, they worked to keep us alive. Especially Dad. As the captain of the ship, he'd been on duty since the cyclone first hit, days ago.

"Got to keep her pointed between the waves. They're coming from all directions. Can't let her capsize or get plowed under by one of those beasts or we're done for," Dad muttered, water dripping from his brown beard.

The adults were slowing down. Staggering, they dropped things, lost their footing, and yelled more and more often. Their eyes drooped, and sometimes they fell asleep for a moment or two, right where they stood. They weren't just tired. They were exhausted beyond anything I'd ever witnessed.

I was surprised when Dad came down for more than a bathroom break. Never before had he quit steering during a storm. Even at mealtimes, he'd stayed there, nibbling on whatever Mom brought him. Now everyone gathered around him.

"We all need sleep. Can't do this any more," Dad yelled, barely audible over the storm.

By the dim light of a swaying kerosene lantern, the crew nodded their heads. Claude, Marie, and Bill stripped off their outerwear and stowed the yellow garments in the hanging locker. Then they trudged toward their respective bunks. Without another word, Claude and Marie disappeared into their private bedroom where Pierre-Paul waited for them. Bill climbed over the canvas curtain onto his bunk on the other side of the galley. He shook his head and muttered something before collapsing into a heap.

Mom and Dad stood over Jolene and me. Dad's lips moved with words I couldn't make out, but I knew he was praying. Pulling up his rain hood, he lifted the kerosene lantern and turned. He trudged up the companionway stairs and out into the storm. Mom grabbed the basket with baby Jackie and followed. She stopped a moment at the top of steps to look back at us, by the light of the lantern, before bolting the door shut. Then she followed Dad as he crossed the cockpit to the aft cabin.

I pulled my fuzzy blue blanket closer, stroking the satiny edge repeatedly, seeking reassurance and comfort.

Everyone was in bed. No one was on deck steering through the storm, keeping those mountainous waves from crashing onto us and pushing us down into the depths of the Indian Ocean, but I trusted my parents. I knew they'd take care of us, even out here so far away from anyone else. I fell asleep, clutching my beloved blankie, as my arms and legs still fought to keep me on the bunk despite the vicious storm. Little did I realize that as the adults lay down exhausted, none of them expected to wake up the next morning, at least not in this life. They were dead tired and couldn't fight any longer.

So how did we end up here, sailing in the middle of the Indian Ocean, fighting this hurricane-strength storm? Let me go back to the beginning, about four months earlier.

Mom, Cheryl, Jolene, and Dad watch a yacht race in Hervey Bay.
"Former Trenton Couple Finds Plenty of Room in Australia."
Trenton Republican-Times, Nov. 17, 1969. Used with permission.

2. The Beginning: Hervey Bay, Australia

"Cast off," Dad yelled, as he stood at the wheel in the cockpit. His thick, dark hair waved in the gentle breeze. His knee-length cotton shorts and light-colored knit shirt were perfect for the sunny autumn day. He smiled and waved to the crowds on the pier, while two men lifted loops of thick, heavy rope over the posts of the dock at either end of the *Berenice*.

A cameraman from the local television station captured the moment on film. A reporter with a microphone in his hands stood beside him. Neighbors and friends waved hands, hats, and handkerchiefs at us.

"Bon voyage!"

"Have a great trip!"

"We'll keep your china safe until you return!"

"See you in a couple of years!"

"Don't forget to write!"

Many faces in the crowd were new to me. Some were patients from Dad's chiropractic practice, here to bid him farewell. Another chiropractor would fix their aches and pains until we returned. How long would that be? Likely three years, Dad guessed when asked.

A local reporter attracted several curious strangers with his numerous newspaper articles and television news stories on the local ABC (Australian Broadcasting Company) station. He'd been intrigued by a professional man, with no prior boat-building experience, who spent two years building a yacht in his spare time with plans to sail with his family around the world. Not just an ordinary yacht either, but a boat made of cement.

Sounds crazy; right? Cement sinks; doesn't it? Dad bought boat-building plans from a British designer, Maurice Griffiths, who claimed his ferro-cement boats were sturdy, not prone to rust like steel ships, nor prone to worms and rot like wooden boats. The chicken-wire framework within would hold broken cement in place if the hull were somehow damaged, and a bag of quick-drying cement could make quick repairs. In England, several ferro-cement boats built from his designs now sailed. However, none had sailed yet in Hervey Bay, a boating town, and people were curious. Maybe some on the jetty were skeptics who came to see if this crazy creation would sink in the harbor.

More than that, locals knew Dad was a chiropractor, not a builder. Did he really plan to sail his entire family around the world in the first boat he ever constructed?

They didn't know it, but before I'd been born, he trained as a surveyor in the United States Air Force. He grew up around tools. He rebuilt cars as a teenager and fixed lots of things around the house. He could read plans and follow directions. As long as he had a decent set of plans, it couldn't be that hard to build an ocean-going vessel; could it?

Of course, he'd need help with construction. He hadn't planned to build it alone. He had friends with training: an electrician, a plumber, and others. Men who were excited about his plans and promised assistance once he started, but who followed through on crazy plans talked about over a few beers? When the time came, his friends were too busy. Or maybe they didn't want this crazy escapade on their conscience when things went wrong. Yet, my stubborn dad didn't quit. Instead, he figured out how to do it himself.

Perhaps some in the crowd were from the hospital in Maryborough, about three hours away. Nurses there wouldn't release six-day-old baby Jackie to go on an insane journey until a former neighbor of ours, a doctor, stepped in.

"Carolyn is one of the best mums I've seen. If she thinks it's safe to take a newborn on that boat, then it must be," he upbraided the nurses.

Other boaters came for the vicarious thrill of seeing a great yachting adventure begin. Some came a few weeks earlier for the launching, when Mom swung a bottle of champagne at the hull, and Dad officially named his creation *Berenice*, meaning "victorious maiden." The name signified his hope for victory over the sea and honored his mother, Grandma Bernice.

From my perch on the top of the companionway, I surveyed the scene. On deck, our crew of two was busy. Richard, a young wiry Australian, hauled in the bowline. Nancy, his pretty wife and a trained teacher, looked up and smiled at the crowd on the dock before pulling on the aft line, the rope at the opposite end of the boat. Dad was reluctant to sail without a crew, even though his hero, Joshua Slocum, sailed the world alone. Richard and Nancy had little sailing experience, but they were willing to work in exchange for a place to sleep, food to eat, and an adventure. Or so they claimed.

Mom opened the slatted doors to the aft cabin, where newborn Jackie cried for a bottle. Jolene played down in the main cabin. Dad stood in the cockpit at the wheel. Altogether, there were seven souls onboard as we left Hervey Bay.

At Dad's order, Richard and Nancy coiled each rope, tied a knot around it, and dropped it through the forward hatch into the sail locker. The putt-putting engine pulled us away from the crowded pier. The sun shone brightly in a cloudless blue sky. With a steady breeze and waves less than a foot high, the day promised an auspicious beginning to our voyage.

As we motored past colorful buoys, catamarans, dinghies, and small yachts of all shapes, the dock gradually shrank in the distance. The wonderful salty smell of the sea air soon gave way to the stench of our diesel engine. The cheers of the crowd were replaced by the loud churning of the engine and its bone-shaking vibrations.

Peace and calm returned soon enough, though. As the crew raised first the mainsail and then the mizzen, Dad shut the engine off. The tranquil sounds of gently flapping sails, cawing seagulls, and lightly splashing waves filled the air.

"Can I come out now?" I pleaded, anxious to get away from the noxious diesel fumes in the cabin. My stomach never traveled well, suffering from carsickness on land and seasickness on water. My roiling stomach would feel better if I sat on the deck, where I could breathe in fresh air. I could lean over the side, if necessary, to avoid making a nasty mess.

"Let me see," Mom said, as she stepped into the cockpit and looked around. Nancy had gone below, muttering to herself. Richard was on deck, standing with his arms akimbo and his head tilted back, as the breeze rustled his hair. Clearly, he'd finished working, too.

"Wally?" Mom asked. "Will the girls be in the way? May they come on deck?" Quiet, unassuming Mom always checked with Dad before doing anything. So, the entire family had been surprised when she insisted that the whole family come with Dad on his planned voyage around the world. He hoped to circumnavigate the globe alone, like Joshua Slocum in *Sailing Alone Around the World*, a book he read long ago in school. As a boy in land-locked Missouri, following Slocum's footsteps seemed impossible, but moving to the coast of Australia changed that.

"Okay, Carolyn, the girls can come up," Dad replied. "Just make sure they stay out of the way." His smile changed to a more serious expression as he looked in my direction and added, "Stay out of the way and don't cause trouble. You'll go right back down if you're in the way. Understood?"

Quietly, I nodded. If Dad said it, he meant business. I didn't want him mad at me. Corporal punishment was commonplace in those days, in schools and homes. Dad wouldn't hesitate to spank a child who disobeyed. As soon as he returned to the business of sailing, I scrambled into the cockpit, and then up and over to the deck.

Scanning the area, I sought the best spot to settle down. I wanted lots of fresh air, away from my dad's stinky cigarette smoke, as well as the diesel-scented cabin air. The stern was out, since Dad was busy there. The main cabin top wouldn't work either, since the main mast was there. The bowsprit could be a problem, too, if Dad wanted to drop anchor or raise the jib. On the starboard side, Richard leaned against a cable securing the main mast and gazed at the sea, but on the port side, several feet from the bowsprit, the deck was empty. Yes, I'd found my spot.

I sank down on my knees. Closing my eyes, I soaked in the warmth of the sun. A light spray moistened my face. I inhaled the fresh, clean salt air. My stomach calmed a little as I lay there, but I didn't feel up to doing anything else. I knew from experience that staying still was the best way to spend the afternoon, best for my stomach.

"Whatcha doing?" Jolene's cheerful voice rang out as she plopped down beside me. She wasn't the least bit seasick. She never was. We'd moved around so much, living in Armidale, New South Wales, then in Maryborough, Queensland and later in nearby Hervey Bay. Neighbors and friends might stay behind, but sisters stayed together as the best of friends. She sat beside me, waited patiently as I pampered my unsettled stomach, and kept me company.

Eventually, I opened my eyes. For the longest time, we sat side by side and quietly gazed at the view. The Australian coastline grew smaller and smaller, fading until it was barely visible. After a while, only a low, fuzzy, gray cloud remained on the horizon. Then suddenly, poof, the cloud vanished and we reached what sailors call "blue water"—water with no land in sight.

Leaning over the edge of the deck, I peered deep into the crystal-clear water. Brightly colored fish darted this way and that. Transparent jellyfish floated along, their tentacles pumping up and down as they meandered about. Large green turtles pulled steadily toward some unseen goal, while steel-gray sharks glided farther below. Creatures darted in and out of the multicolored coral's myriad holes in what seemed a playful game of hide-and-seek. The peacefulness of the scene soaked in and soothed my stomach, eased my nerves, and calmed my spirit.

Petite Jolene played quietly at my side with her favorite brown-haired doll. She bounced the doll on her knee or on the deck, and together we quietly whiled away the afternoon.

"Lower the mainsail!" Dad bellowed, scooting off his perch on the aft cabin where he'd sat with one hand on the tiller. He jumped into the cockpit and grabbed the wheel instead. The wheel, which was next to the mounted compass and the engine controls, was better than the lever-like tiller for steering through close quarters.

"Right. I'll be there in a few." Lanky Richard sauntered over to loosen the line to the large mainsail. The rope had been wrapped figure-eight fashion around a cleat on the larger mast.

"I don't see why I have to do any more work. I was just about to paint my nails," his wife, Nancy muttered, before she ambled over and helped guide the large sail.

"Careful, don't tangle the line," Dad warned.

"Why doesn't he make his wife come help?" Nancy asked under her breath, ignoring the fact that Mom had just been released from the hospital and now cared for a newborn.

With a little more coaching, they managed to drop the sail in pleats onto the wooden boom and furl it securely until the sail was needed again.

Most of the afternoon was gone. Ahead of us on the horizon, what appeared to be a low fuzzy cloud grew larger and larger. Eventually it took solid form, transforming into an island with a lush green jungle-covered mountain in the middle. Well, maybe it was only a large hill, but it looked mountainous to a girl who'd grown up along the coast.

"Belay that line!" Dad pointed to a flapping rope. Sailors never tied ropes; they belayed lines. Such words were one way to tell a sailor from a landlubber. I wasn't a sailor girl yet, but I was working on it, even though Dad thought I was too little to do any of the exciting stuff onboard.

"Hmmph." Nancy looked around and rolled her eyes, before she ambled over to the rope.

Dad's face reddened. He hurled his spent cigarette butt into the sea and slammed his hand onto the wheel. He usually saved his hand-rolled cigarette butts to salvage the tobacco left in them for a new cigarette. At sea, we reused everything possible, including the nasty cigarettes.

I knew Dad was fuming, but apparently, Nancy didn't. He'd yelled an order, and she'd taken her sweet time following it. As captain of the ship, he wanted orders obeyed immediately, not because he was mean, but because lives might depend on it. If he were that mad at me, I'd expect a spanking, but he didn't even raise his voice to her, which may have been a big mistake.

Once the rope was secured, Dad pulled the starter knob. With a snort, the engine roared to life.

"Cheryl, get down below," ordered Mom, scurrying past me. "Take Jolene with you. Keep an eye on her."

"Okay." I grabbed Jolene's hand and we hurried, taking the long way around to stay out of Dad's way. Back down in the main cabin, the putrid smell of diesel hit me full-force again. The taste of bile hit my mouth. I longed to stay in the fresh air, but knew I couldn't.

Watching the view calmed my stomach earlier, so I tried to look out the high oval portholes. I strained my neck to see the blue sky through them, but that didn't help. I couldn't perch in the companionway, peering out the cabin door, and watch Jolene, too. Sighing, I plopped on the floor and beckoned to my sister. Wedged between a galley berth and the drop-leaf table, there wasn't much room, but I hoped the stench would be less potent here. I settled down to read a book aloud.

We left a lot of things behind when we moved onboard. My bicycle, most of my toys, books, and clothes simply wouldn't fit in our 39-foot long yacht. So, I brought along only a few special possessions, ones I wouldn't soon tire of. Plastic interlocking blocks could build a variety of toys to play with. A few dolls and handful of good books were stored in the leeboard, the curtain-like piece of canvas that tucked under the berth's mattress and kept us from falling out.

I read to her from *Digit Dick on the Great Barrier Reef*, an Australian children's storybook about a thumb-sized boy who ends up on the bottom of the reef with the creatures who live there. That is, I tried to read it, but the story was too long for Jolene. Besides, the pounding noise, unending vibrations, and ghastly stench of the engine attacked my head, making it difficult for me to see the words on the page. In the end, I set the book down and climbed to the nearby upper berth that would be my bed at night, and curled up, clutching my aching stomach. I watched as Jolene sat on the lower bunk, just in front of mine, looking at the pictures in the book, pictures much like the view we'd enjoyed earlier.

By late afternoon, we anchored in a small island harbor. Fishing boats, a triple-hulled trimaran, rowboats, sailing vessels with one or two masts, as well as various motor boats bobbed about the harbor. Stinkpots, that's what Dad called the sail-less motor boats. After being cooped up in the cabin as the motor fumed, the nickname made sense. Some of the boats in the harbor were shiny, new-looking boats with fresh coats of paint, while others had peeling paint, patches, rust spots, and other evidence of a hard, long life. Colorful buoys bobbed up and down, marking the channel into the harbor or warning of areas where hidden dangers could shred the hull of a stray vessel.

Some boats were empty, waiting for their inhabitants to return. Others were occupied by people who seemed settled for the night. Hmmm, they must live on their boats, too. Funny, I'd never thought of boats as homes before. Boats were for transportation or fun. Now I realized that, for a lot of people, just like us, boats were home. We'd entered a new community.

"Hey, look at those kids. On that boat," I said to Jolene as I stood on her berth and looked through a porthole.

"I can't see anyone," she said, as she sat quietly playing.

"Out the window," I said, but then realized that she wouldn't be able to see them even if she stood on the bunk. I could barely see them myself, and she was shorter.

I turned around and waved to them. They waved back. I could see that they said something, too, but I couldn't hear them, so I made some silly hand signals. They laughed and made funny faces at me. Friends didn't seem hard to find, out here on the water, so far from our old beach house and friends.

My stomach felt much better now that the *Berenice* was moored. While the yacht still swayed and rocked with the waves, the motion was gentler than when we'd moved through the water. The two hatches were propped open, and a light breeze flowed through the main cabin, chasing away the diesel fumes and making a chart flutter. The pressure in my head lifted as the air cleared. The pounding in my brain abated, as the gentle lapping of tiny waves washing against the hull brought back the peaceful feeling I enjoyed on the deck earlier.

"What's that?" Jolene asked.

"Don't know." I'd heard it, too. I jumped off the berth and ran to the doorway to get a better view.

"Dad and Richard are lowering the dinghy," I said, as Jolene came over to see for herself.

Through the open doorway, I saw Dad and Richard lower the rowboat from its storage frame on the rear of the *Berenice*. With a splash, it hit the water below. Dad descended first. Then Richard followed. Both disappeared from view as they sat. With a few creaking and splashing sounds, the white dinghy then reappeared a few feet away. Richard sat in the stern, with his back to me. Dad sat on the center bench facing me. Hunched over, his body rhythmically swayed back and forth, as he lifted the oars through the air, and then pulled them down through the water. Tugging with his entire body, he pulled the dinghy away from the *Berenice*.

"Where are they going?" I asked Mom, as she carried Jackie in her Moses basket through the cockpit toward their aft cabin. I followed partway and sat on a cockpit bench.

"Oh, to take care of some errands." She climbed down into the aft cabin where my parents and baby Jackie would sleep. Placing the newborn on the double bed, she unpinned her dirty diaper and stowed it in a bucket until Mom did laundry. Grabbing a square of white terry cloth, she quickly folded it and pinned the clean diaper in place.

I watched the men in the distance. They climbed from the dinghy to a pier, chatted briefly with two chaps who stood on the shore holding fishing poles. Then Dad and Richard hurried down the road.

The pier was a busy place. Some men moved wooden boxes off a ship and stacked them on the pier, while others moved the pile of crates closer to the road. Another fellow sat on the deck of a moored boat, a large pile of fabric around him, his hands busily moving back and forth, as he made repairs of some kind. Another held a bucket; his head and shoulders bobbed up and down, as he reached into the bucket regularly. A couple of others stood facing each other, hands gesturing, apparently discussing something.

"Doing anything fun?" Jolene's voice startled me, as she dropped down on the deck near me.

"Just looking around. Seeing what's here." I shrugged.

"Hmmm . . . It's different; isn't it?"

"Yes." I sighed as I thought of Hervey Bay and our beach house on stilts. Allen, a friend about my age, lived a few houses down. He was probably running around his yard or riding his bike. Our next-door neighbor was likely working in her garden. My sister and I stayed with her when Mom had to remain in bed for the unborn baby's sake. She served the most delicious garden-fresh beets, warm with butter. A narrow road and a steep plant-covered sandy hill separated our front yard from the Pacific Ocean. We spent a lot of time playing on the beach or watching yachts race, but that seemed a world away now.

Shaking my head to clear the melancholy thoughts that threatened to erupt, I concentrated again on the view before us. Beyond the harbor, the pier, the road, and the gray weatherworn wooden buildings, trees, vines, and all sorts of greenery covered the mountain. I squinted, looking for details in that massive mound of green.

"Do you think people live up there?" I asked.

"I don't know." Jolene's wavy hair bounced slightly as she shrugged her shoulders. "Maybe."

We stared at the jungle for several minutes.

"Do you think any kids live up there?" I didn't expect her to know the answer. I stretched and shifted position to get comfortable on the cockpit bench. We both stared a while longer.

"Is that part of a roof in amongst the greenery?" I pointed to a spot that seemed a different color.

"Maybe. Or maybe it's a tree," Jolene replied, as she picked up her doll again.

"I think maybe there are. Kids living there, I mean," I murmured after a while, answering my own question. "Do they go to school? Or dress like us? I wonder what they eat." I tried to imagine how our lives would change if we lived in that mysterious mountain jungle, but I never found the answers to my questions. From our new floating home, I just watched and wondered.

The next morning, we raised our anchor and set sail for the next island on the Great Barrier Reef. So many little islands and harbors dot the eastern Australian coast that we sailed from one to another, spending each night safely moored. We stayed a day or two, long enough to get a good night's rest and do any necessary business on shore. The men rowed ashore and chatted with the locals, bought fuel, filled our water tanks, or made occasional repairs. Often we ate dinner with a local official who wanted to practice his English or was excited to meet someone new, or we enjoyed a meal at a local restaurant for some fresh fare. Mom took us along to the local laundry facility or the market.

At each island we visited, I gazed at the jungle in the center and imagined exploring and discovering what was there.

Inevitably, Mom would call, "Cheryl! What's the matter? Pay attention." Her voice would bring me back to reality.

Maybe someday I'd get to explore, but I didn't hold out much hope. Mom and Dad saved money for years, pinching pennies to afford to build a seaworthy yacht. They saved so we could buy the necessary supplies and live off our savings as we traveled. Dad didn't want to dawdle along the way. Dawdling might waste money. Like a lot of blue-water sailors, Dad focused on the goal, on sailing the globe, rather than on savoring the details along the way. Mom, on the other hand, was just along for the ride. Sailing the globe wasn't her childhood dream. Having a family that stayed together was her dream, so she kept her family fed, safe, in clean clothes, and together. Seeing much of the world beyond our boat seemed unlikely.

Little did I know that I would soon explore a deserted tropical island. I'd trek into its jungle and discover something that scientists thousands of miles away would report to the world.

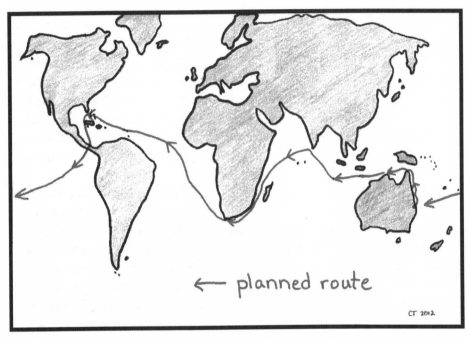

The route we intended to sail on our journey around the world.

3. CREW TROUBLES

"I know. I know," Dad growled, shaking his head as he paced the deck a few weeks later.

The *Berenice* was moored in another Australian harbor farther north. Mom, who rarely spoke up, started the discussion as soon as Richard and Nancy left to go sightseeing on shore. Mom had had enough.

"What am I supposed to do? We need a crew, and they're the only crew we've got right now," Dad said. Shoving his hands into the pockets of his knee-length khaki shorts, he stopped pacing for a moment. He'd grown a beard since razors and saltwater didn't work well together. He still wore his black-rimmed glasses, but the knee-high socks he used to wear rarely made an appearance anymore. Bare feet worked better onboard a boat where dampness got into everything.

Mom and Dad were in the cockpit. I spied on them through the open doorway at the top of the companionway ladder. They weren't happy, and I didn't want them getting mad at me, but I wanted to hear their discussion. I didn't worry so much about Mom getting mad at me; Dad was another story. Mom was predictable, but I hadn't figured out how to tell when Dad reached his limit and was about to lose his temper. Still, I listened intently since I was part of the reason Mom wanted to get rid of Nancy.

Dad cocked his head, gazing at the sea. After a few minutes, he spoke again. "Maybe we could do it without a crew. I don't know. Day sailing isn't the same as blue-water sailing." His voice trailed off.

"But, Wally," Mom repeated, "What good is a crew that doesn't do the job?"

Dad wasn't happy with Richard and Nancy either. A good crew readily goes to work when needed, but ours relaxed as much as they could. They helped when pushed, but Dad was tired of pushing, and tired of filling in when they didn't do the job. Mom was more upset.

"Cheryl's been out of school for weeks now," she reminded Dad. "When is Nancy going to start teaching her? That was part of our agreement, but

Nancy acts as though work is beneath her. It wouldn't be that much work. Cheryl can read and figure out most of the work herself."

"I know."

"Besides, Wally, I'm tired of Nancy's whining. She doesn't give me any consideration for busy with the baby or making meals. She's so afraid she'll do a little extra work," Mom snapped.

I'd been in second grade in Hervey Bay, which might seem odd for a six-and-a-half-year-old, but I hadn't skipped grades or anything. Grades and ages just matched up differently in Australia than they do elsewhere, I guess.

I liked school, even though my teacher had been a bit crazy. Why else would a woman ban erasers from her classroom? She told us on the first day of school last January that cheaters used erasers to rub out wrong answers after they peeked at another student's paper. If we brought a pencil with an eraser attached, we were to have her pop off the eraser. If we didn't . . . Well, she never said exactly what would happen, but I'd seen students slapped with a ruler. I didn't want to go there. We couldn't even cross out an answer. Crossing out was as bad as erasing.

Despite her craziness, I loved school. I liked the desks built for two students that required seatmates to work together to get their supplies. Even when we couldn't use the playground equipment, I liked playing hopscotch or house on the asphalt with the other girls, while the boys played football or other ball games in the nearby paddock. Mostly, I liked learning new things and trying to teach them to my little sister.

Yet, not going to school was even better. I'd gotten my sea legs, so the seasickness was gone, but I still loved sitting on the deck, watching the creatures of the Great Barrier Reef and telling stories to my sister. I loved reading books just for fun, playing with our colorful plastic blocks for hours on end, or playing make-believe with our dolls. More than anything, I loved the relaxed, carefree feeling of taking each day as it came, of sitting when I felt like it or standing if I preferred, of eating a snack when I was hungry, rather than following orders constantly. I hoped Nancy never got around to teaching me.

"I'll figure something out," Dad said in a tone that said he didn't want to discuss the matter further.

We spent a few days at the next port, somewhere on the mainland of northeastern Australia. Was it Cairns? I couldn't keep track of the different harbors. Usually, we stayed a night or two and sailed off the next morning. When we stayed longer than that, it was best to stay out of Dad's way. He slammed things around, and our slightest mistake would end with one of us in big, big trouble.

Why? Staying longer meant the *Berenice* needed repairs, again. It wasn't that the *Berenice* was poorly built. Despite Dad building her himself, she was a beautiful yacht—if I do say so myself. Glistening white, with strips of gorgeous woodwork marking the water line on the sides, the hull didn't look clunky as one might expect of cement. It was sleek and graceful. The woodwork of the cabin sides and bulwarks gleamed with a beautiful reddish hue and looked polished to perfection, unlike some of the graying weathered boats I'd seen. Her two wooden masts rose tall and proud from the forward ends of each cabin. Everyone who came aboard commented on what a beauty the *Berenice* was. Despite the constant traveling for several weeks now, Dad's work hadn't fallen apart. That wasn't the problem.

True, the head tended to smell musty, and Mom complained it was impossible to keep mold and mildew out of it. Dad blamed a design in which the entire bathroom doubled as a shower stall. The problem lessened once we learned to shower on shore in the public facilities most harbors offer. However, other sailors shrugged and blamed the wet sea air, saying every boat faced the same problem.

No, the problem wasn't Dad's workmanship. Rather, the problem was the diesel engine that didn't like the moist salt air, or the fuel it was given, or something. We didn't use it much because most of the time sails powered the *Berenice*, but getting in and out of harbors without an engine was tricky. At sea, the boat could be turned to best catch the wind, zigzagging at times to eventually head the desired direction. In a harbor, where a small river-like channel was the only safe path, with boats, rocks and other dangers to dodge, engine power was necessary, so each morning as we sailed out of a harbor, and each late afternoon as we sailed into the next, Dad turned the ignition to start the engine. That is, he tried to. Sometimes it started just fine, but often it protested, coughing and bucking. After a few false starts, it might begin but sometimes it simply refused. Then Dad would hail another vessel to tow us, if possible. If not, he cautiously sailed in with a lot of starts and stops as he waited for the wind to cooperate, retracing our path and starting over again at times, until we made it to an anchorage.

Staying in a harbor for a few days had good points and bad. A longer stay made it more likely I could go ashore to run off energy, talk to other sailors, or take a stroll with Mom. Besides worrying about Dad's temper, there was another drawback. Unlike the rest of the family, I quickly lost my sea legs if we moored for a few days, so I faced three days of seasickness after each extended stay.

How many times had we stopped to fix the engine? I'd lost count, but Dad's complaints about the time and money the engine cost had turned to "I hate this bloody thing!" He slammed tools, kicked the engine, or punched the engine's access panel.

I wasn't surprised when he stomped off the *Berenice*. He jerked the lines that held the dinghy, slammed the oarlocks into place with loud clanks, and whapped his hands against the side of our yacht as he pushed off to go ashore again. However, I was surprised later when Nancy and Richard stormed out of their bedroom in the forward end of the main cabin, juggling armloads of baggage. They glared but said nothing as they loaded their goods onto the dinghy. Apparently, Dad had decided what to do about them.

In their place, three scrawny young men, in their early twenties, came aboard. I watched, wondering if one of them would be my new teacher. With grins on their faces and buoyant steps, they were nothing like our previous crew. They eagerly went to work, happy to be at sea, bartering their work for an adventure. Well, two of them did anyway.

"Ohhh," moaned Jeff, as he writhed on one of the blue vinyl-covered mattresses Mom had sewn for the berths. His face a pasty green, he clutched his stomach. He tossed and turned, groaned some more, and curled into a fetal position.

"Come on, Jeff. Try getting some fresh air," one of his friends urged.

"Uggh," Jeff replied, as each grabbed an arm, and together they lifted him off the berth. With their help, he shuffled up on deck. Slouched over the railing, his head drooping to his chest, he looked as wretched as a dilapidated half-eaten dog toy.

I looked up from where I sat on the opposite side of the deck, with my head hanging over the side, since I'd lost my sea legs. "You'll feel better in a few days," I reassured him.

The fresh air and sunshine didn't help him. He moaned more and couldn't stand without help from a buddy. No one else in my family or our previous crew had been seasick, so it felt odd to have company in my misery.

"Ohh. Down," he groaned.

"What's that, mate?" his friend asked, leaning closer to catch the words. "You want back down?"

"Mmm," was the only reply, but his friends helped him, practically carried him, back to his berth below.

Three days later, I felt fine, as I knew I would. Three was the magic number for me. If we anchored for three days, I lost my sea legs, but I earned them back in three days of sailing.

Yet, Jeff still lay on his berth, moaning, groaning, and clutching his stomach. At the urging of his buddies, he pulled himself off the bunk and shuffled up on deck.

"He'll be fine in a few days," Dad assured his buddies. "Give him time to adjust. Some people take longer than others."

A week later, Jeff still looked green. He was thinner and paler, his skin almost gray. His eyes sunk into his skull. He rarely rose from his bed.

His friends lost their bounce and grins. They were quieter and exchanged lots of anxious glances.

A few days later, as Dad drank his morning coffee, his eyes suddenly popped open. His body jerked. I wasn't sure what had just happened, but as he slammed his cup down, spilling coffee out onto the galley table, I knew not to ask. Bolting up, he scooted around the table, which had one leaf folded down to leave more space in the galley. Dad grabbed something from a bunk and stormed out of the cabin.

I looked at Jolene, raised my eyebrows, and nodded in Dad's direction. She shrugged her shoulders and took another bite of cereal.

The sound of Dad's heavy footsteps on the deck above our heads stopped abruptly. The crewmen were on deck, drinking their coffee in the early morning air, waiting for us to cast off and set sail. Most of Dad's angry words were loud enough to be understood down below.

"I said no drugs, and I meant it! I don't know which of you this belongs to, but he'd better be gone in an hour. I don't need that kind of trouble on my yacht."

Moments later, the three men crowded into the forward bedroom. They spoke in muffled tones, though I caught the words "shouldn't have done it on Thursday Island" and "worse on Prince of Wales Island."

Cabinet doors slammed, and belongings whapped against the berths. Within minutes, the three hustled out of the cabin, hauling their duffel bags. They didn't make eye contact as they scurried off the boat.

With her eyebrows drawn together, Mom tilted her head in Dad's direction. "What on earth are we going to do now? Stay and look for a new crew?"

"No! We're getting away from here, now. I don't want to be within a cooee of them and any trouble they've got. Last thing we need is to lose the *Berenice* for their crimes. We'll have to go it alone and look for a new crew when we get to Darwin."

Mom looked at me and muttered something about school. I wasn't sure what she said, but I was pretty sure my leisure days were numbered.

Dad popped up on deck, raised the anchor, and turned on the engine faster than ever before. I fed two-month-old Jackie a bottle of formula as Mom helped sail the *Berenice* out of the harbor.

They planned to find a new crew later. There were always people hanging around harbors looking to make a deal for a cruise. Finding a crew wasn't hard; finding a good crew was the problem. We wanted a better crew than the two we'd had so far, a crew that would work willingly, be reasonably healthy, and stay out of trouble with the law.

Little did we know that, despite my parents' best efforts, the next crew would bring more trouble—especially for Jolene and me.

4. Disaster at School

We sailed into Darwin in Australia's Northern Territory two months after beginning our voyage more than 2,000 miles away. We arrived with just our family of five, but Dad wouldn't leave Darwin without a crew to share the workload, to help keep the yacht on course and safe on the long journey across the ocean.

Before leaving continental Australia, we needed immunizations for international travel—including shots for illnesses, such as smallpox and cholera, that were required in only a few remote countries. We didn't want to be refused admittance to any port because of health requirements. We awaited Jackie's official birth certificate, since we couldn't update our passports without it, and we loaded up on supplies, including enough food and water to last for many weeks.

With so much to do, I wasn't surprised when Mom woke us early the next morning.

"Come on, get dressed. Hurry," she said, handing both Jolene and me a short cotton dress rather than our usual swimming togs or shorts. Baby Jackie was already dressed in a pastel dress with bloomers over her cotton diaper. "And put these on," she added, handing us our sandals. We never wore shoes out at sea.

"Don't dawdle," Mom ordered as she set a bowl of Sugar Smacks in front of each of us. Mom had given up on cornflakes and other boring healthy cereal, since Jolene and I refused to eat them with reconstituted powdered milk, the only milk we could manage without refrigeration.

"Move along. Get going." Mom carried two-month-old Jackie, while Jolene and I hurried to keep up.

"Where are we going?" I asked.

"Right there," she pointed to a bus stop sign.

She spoke briefly to the bus driver, handed him some money, and motioned for us to sit down.

I looked around the interior of the bus at the various passengers, dark-skinned aborigines, men dressed for the office, and women heading to the market.

Up one street and down another we went, until the driver turned and said, "This is your stop, Ma'am. Just head down that way." He pointed, and added, "You'll soon see it. Can't miss the sign."

We hadn't gone far when Mom said, "Ah, there it is." Mom nodded her head at a building bearing a sign "Larrakeyah Primary School."

I looked at Mom and then back at the building. With a sigh, I realized this was Mom's solution to the school problem.

"How long do I have to go here?"

"You've missed two months of school already," Mom said, in a tone that brooked no nonsense. "Until we figure something else out, you'll go to school here." Her tone softened and she added, "I'm not sure how long it will be. Probably a few weeks."

Mom spoke with the headmistress and filled out some forms. Then turning to me, she said, "Be good. Have a good day." Taking Jolene by the hand, she carried Jackie out the door, leaving me with the headmistress.

Yesterday, I sailed the ocean, spending my time as I pleased. Now, I felt a bit queasy. My stomach had grown used to the constant rocking of the boat. I still felt the swaying of the boat underneath me, as though the land were moving. In fact, I felt land sick—if that's the opposite of seasick. Plus, my head spun with the unexpectedness of being suddenly thrust into school.

The headmistress led me through the school, talking and pointing as we went along.

Why wasn't I warned of this? Why wasn't I told I'd start school here?

I nodded as she said something about catching a bus at the end of the day, but my thoughts and the queer sensations within me blocked out most of her words.

"Cheryl!" The headmistress glared at me. She must have said something important. I didn't want to be trouble, so I inhaled deeply to clear my head, and I concentrated on her words.

"You'll be in Miss Smythe's Year II class." She opened a door and introduced me to the woman inside the room.

A couple of dozen children raised their heads to look at me. Unlike my old school in Hervey Bay, these students sat at individual desks arranged in orderly rows facing the blackboard.

"You may sit in the last seat of that row." My new teacher pointed to a row in the center of the room. "In my class, it is a privilege to sit in the back of the row. Students who misbehave sit in the front." She bent down to peer at my face. "Be sure you don't lose the right to sit there," she added sternly, shaking a finger at me.

I walked down the aisle carrying the pile of books she'd given me. I didn't want trouble with her or my parents, so I resolved to remain in that seat of honor. After putting my books away, I straightened up and looked around the room. The other children chatted quietly. Most of them looked my way periodically, so I guessed they were talking about me.

Through the hubbub, I heard Miss Smythe speaking. "Open your math books to page . . ." Rustling papers and the sounds of books opening increased the noise level. I couldn't understand the rest of her words.

I found the math book and set it on the desk. Peeking at a nearby girl's book, I couldn't make out the page number. I leaned over and whispered, "Which page did she say?"

Silence enveloped the room at the same moment. My whisper filled the silence and echoed through the room. Every head in the room whirled to face me. I froze, only my eyes moved, as I looked this way and that. I tried to figure out what had happened. I'd missed something. Something important.

"Cheryl! Come up here. Immediately!" the teacher ordered, grabbing a ruler from her large wooden desk. Her smile was gone, replaced by a glare and clenched jaw.

Nervously, I marched up to her desk, past rows of silent children. Several lowered their heads to stare at their desks.

What had I done? What was about to happen?

"Hold out your hand," Miss Smythe demanded in a brisk tone, brandishing a ruler.

She grabbed my hand and turned it over, palm upward. Whack! I winced and stood there, a red mark across my hand, mortified in front of this class of strangers.

"Go back to your desk." She waved the ruler at the rest of the class and added, "Let this be a warning to all. When I say quiet, I mean it."

Now I understood. I must have whispered my question just as she threatened to punish the next one to make a noise. Biting my lip, I trudged back to my desk with tears running down my face.

I hoped she wouldn't tell my parents. I'd never gotten in trouble at school before. I was sure my dad would be mad at me for disrupting class and not listening. I'd likely get a spanking at home, too.

For the rest of the day, I forced myself to pay attention and avoid further trouble. Never again would I ask a question of another student. In fact, I wouldn't ask a question of the teacher, either, unless absolutely necessary, but I kept wondering whether she would tell my parents.

The sound of the bell at the end of the day was a relief. I plodded behind the other students, following them outside. Then I stopped. How was I supposed to get home? The headmistress had said something about catching a bus. Looking around, I saw some buses and wandered over to them.

"Come on. Get on your bus, young lady. They're ready to leave," an irritated voice barked from behind me.

I didn't want the bus to leave without me, and I didn't want to get in trouble again, so I followed orders as best I could. I climbed onto the nearest bus and sat in an empty seat.

How would I know where to get off? I considered asking the driver for help, but he'd ask my address, and I wouldn't know what to say. I didn't know the name of our marina. I couldn't even describe it. We'd just arrived and all the harbors from the past couple of months were a jumble in my brain. Perhaps I'd spot the *Berenice* as the bus drove past, so I stared out the window, hoping to see the harbor and our boat. However, the bus drove up and down residential streets, streets full of houses, not boats. Streets that didn't look at all familiar.

"Why are you still here?" the bus driver demanded, startling me.

Looking around, I realized the bus was empty. The bus must have finished its route, but I'd never seen our yacht. The bus driver stood over me demanding answers. A bad day had gotten worse.

"Ummm, I don't know." I tried to hold back my tears. Dad teased me sometimes for crying too easily.

"You don't know? Where do you live?" he demanded.

"I don't know," I repeated, tears rolling down my face.

"Which bus were you supposed to be on?"

"I don't know," I said again, shrugging my shoulders.

His eyebrows mashed together across his forehead as he stared at me. Then shaking his head, he said, "Guess I'll have to take you back to school and let them figure it out." Muttering about wasted time, he strode to the front of the bus, sat down, and started the engine.

As we drew near the school, I saw the headmistress speaking to Mom. Jackie was in her arms and Jolene at her side. I wiped my eyes and tried to stop sobbing. Mom was here. Everything would be all right.

"Well, here she is," the headmistress snapped as the driver opened the door for me. Turning to my mother, she added, "Thank goodness she had sense enough to return."

"Where were you? I've been so worried! Why didn't you wait for me? You knew I was coming on the city bus to get you." Mom shook a finger at me, but then squeezed me with a hug.

I didn't mind the scolding. I was so glad she found me. This had been the worst day ever. I never wanted to come back to this school again, ever. However, as bad as the day had been, no one told my parents about the trouble I'd been in earlier. At least not yet. I couldn't wait to leave this place. Surely, nothing could be worse than this day; could it?

5. Good-bye, Australia

After a month in Darwin, we were ready to leave Australia and head to Indochina. The hospital had poked and prodded us, and our immunizations were up-to-date. The engine was overhauled, again. Parts were replaced and the engine completely rebuilt, so it shouldn't give us any more trouble.

Jackie now shared an Australian passport with Jolene. My parents and I shared a new American passport, since we'd been born there. My sisters could have had American passports, too, since our parents were Americans, but a lot of people were mad at the United States. Dad figured it was safer to have at least one passport from a country with few enemies. Besides, Australia was our adopted home, even though Dad wasn't ready to give up his American citizenship for Australian. My sisters' Aussie document made it simpler to fly the flag with the Southern Cross and Union Jack legally, as well as to register the *Berenice* as an Australian ship.

The *Berenice* was packed full of supplies. The storage areas underneath the berths were stuffed with boxes of powdered milk, jars of Vegemite sandwich spread, massive sacks of flour and rice, huge bags of potatoes, sugar, salt and other staples. Cans of baby formula, golden syrup, tuna, steak and kidney pie, and vegetables were stacked in the remaining storage space. We had enough food to last for months. Diesel filled the fuel tank. Boxlike tins contained kerosene for our lanterns and stove. Both 130-gallon water tanks were full of drinkable water.

Obviously, we didn't need to stock up on saltwater, though we'd use it along the way, too. The head and the galley each had two faucets. Like old-fashioned farm pumps, each faucet's lever was pumped up and down repeatedly to get water. Instead of hot and cold taps, we had fresh and salt-water faucets. We used seawater as much as possible, for washing or for cooking in recipes calling for salted water, to conserve our potable water supply.

Dad pulled Mom aside. "I may have found a new crew. A nice family. Marie's French, and Claude's a New Zealander. Their four-year-old should give the girls a playmate. They're willing to pay to get to South Africa." Another captain warned that he'd erred by not charging previous crews for the ride.

"So, what's wrong?" Mom asked. Dad usually made plans without asking Mom's opinion, so she knew something was up.

"For one thing, they met an Aussie, Bill, and now they want to include him in the deal. They just met the bloke, but he seems a quiet, friendly bloke." Dad paused for a moment, and then said, "A couple of old salts predicted trouble if we bring him, too. He'd have to bunk in the galley without privacy. It's a long journey. Likely be days or weeks at sea with nowhere to get away from each other." He stared past the ships in the harbor and stroked his beard.

"Do what you think best, dear," Mom said. "But a little friend for the girls would be nice, and a family isn't likely to be get into trouble like the last crew."

"There's more, though. The boy was raised by a string of nannies and a rich French grandma. Apparently his dad—not Claude, he must be the stepdad—is a Peruvian Indian, and there's some Peruvian law that prevents kids—or maybe people in general—with Native American blood from leaving their country."

"You mean they smuggled their own child out of Peru?" Mom asked.

"Looks that way, but they've got a proper-looking passport for him. Someone in the family works for the Peruvian government. They say the passport's legit. What do you think? I don't want to take on problems with the law."

"You're sure there's not more to the story? Did their passports clear customs?"

"In Australia and New Zealand both. They've got the stamps to prove it." Dad checked the passports himself.

"Doesn't sound like it'll be a problem, since we aren't heading to Peru. No one else is going to care about it," Mom said slowly. She didn't like seeing a family separated without just cause.

In the end, dark-haired Pierre-Paul—or Pear-Paw, as Jolene and I called him—and his graceful brunette young mother, Marie, and serious curly-haired stepfather, Claude, took up residence in the front bedroom. With bunks designed to sleep two, the quarters were cramped for a family of three, but they rejected the empty berth available in the galley. They wanted to be together as a family.

Everything was in tip-top shape. We were ready to head into the vast unknown, to travel the world to distant countries, to leave the country that had been our home since I was six months old. The real excitement was about to begin.

I was glad to get away from Larrakeyah Primary School, though the rest of the month had been better than the beginning. Miss Smythe never told my parents about the trouble I caused. She must have understood what happened, because she didn't move me to another seat and never spoke of the incident again. Of course, I was careful after that to direct every question to her and only her. I never spoke without permission, and I learned how to get home from school.

Enthusiastically, I waved good-bye to everyone on the dock. Out of the harbor, a familiar churning struck my stomach. We'd been in the harbor a month, and I'd lost my sea legs, but even the stench of the vibrating diesel engine didn't dampen my spirits as mainland Australia shrank in the distance behind us.

"This makes it official," Dad said, as he wrote "Log of the Yacht BERENICE" on the cover of an orange exercise book. Inside the notebook, he inscribed, "28 August 1971. Left Fannie Bay, Darwin at 14.05 hrs. bound for Christmas Island with 8 souls and myself aboard."

Day sailing was over. Christmas Island was about 1800 miles away, two hundred miles south of Indonesia. It would take much more than a day to sail that far.

"Mom, is it Christmas all the time on Christmas Island?" I imagined an island where Christians opened presents every day and ended every supper with crackers. Not edible crackers, but the kind that pop open. Cardboard tubes covered with colorful paper were an Australian tradition for holidays and birthdays. Pulling the paper on each end caused a cracking sound as the cracker opened and revealed small candies, toys or other treats.

"No, dear." Mom chuckled as she fixed a bottle for three-month-old Jackie. "It was discovered on Christmas Day long ago. That's where the name came from."

Hmmm, that wasn't as exciting, but I still hoped Christmas Island would be fun to visit.

As soon as the engine was off and the hustle and bustle died down, I hurried on deck. I craved the fresh clean sea air that eased my nausea. Jolene and Pierre-Paul followed, but instead of sitting calmly, they ran around the deck, laughing and playing. I paid them little attention as I gazed at the ocean, watching the waves and the sea creatures below, though there were fewer here than on the Great Barrier Reef off eastern Australia. The water off northern Australia wasn't crystal clear, either, but it was still soothing to watch nature, looking for signs of life.

"Aggh!" A shriek pierced the air. Looking around I saw Jolene, with her hands on her cheeks, eyes opened wide as olives. She must be the screamer.

"What's wrong?" I jumped up, intending to help if I could.

"My doll! My doll!" She pointed into the ocean below where she stood.

A tiny plastic doll, about two inches tall, with a tiny transparent zippered carrying case, was given to Jolene in Darwin. She showed the doll to everyone she met. She played with it for hours, putting it in and out of the case, undressing and dressing it repeatedly, but now, her beloved doll floated briskly past the *Berenice*.

Pierre-Paul laughed as he skipped along the deck toward the stern, following the doll as it floated past. I watched until the doll disappeared over a small wave. It reappeared on the crest of the next wave, only to disappear once more, forever.

"What's going on?" Mom popped her head out of the entrance to the aft cabin where she'd been changing a diaper. Three-month-old Jackie slept there, snug in her basket, most of each day, lulled to sleep by the constant rocking motion and the soft shushing lullaby of the sea racing along our hull.

Jolene tried to explain, but hiccupping sobs punctuated the words.

"Quit crying, so I can understand you," Mom ordered in a kind, no-nonsense tone.

After a couple more wails, Jolene took two deep breaths. Then she tried again. "Pear-Paw grabbed my doll." She pursed her lips and glared over at him. "He threw it overboard, into the water. It's back there!" She pointed to where we'd last seen the tiny doll.

Gently Mom said, "Even if I could see it and it still floated, you know we can't go back and get it. If we turned the *Berenice* around, we'd never find it. The doll's gone. I'm sorry, honey."

Jolene understood. She threw one of her own toys overboard long ago, but once she realized the toy was lost forever, she never tried that again.

Mom hugged her and told her to calm down. Then she turned to Pierre-Paul and said, "I'm sure you won't do that again." Then she returned downstairs.

Pierre-Paul grinned and danced a little jig. He hadn't apologized and didn't seem sorry. Maybe he was just excited about being at sea. Maybe he was exploring, learning how things worked out here so far from land and the life he'd known. I hoped he learned a lesson and wouldn't throw anything else overboard. Little did I know that was only the beginning of trouble with Pierre-Paul.

6. School at Sea

"Cheryl!" Mom called from the galley. She pointed to the berth beside the galley table. With one leaf folded down, the table was half its full size.

A pile of books sat on the table with a pencil, some notebook paper, and a set of four or five stapled pages lay beside them. Curiously, I looked at the first of the stapled typewritten sheets. The words "Queensland Primary Correspondence School" stood out. I glanced over at Mom and then at the books. There were a social studies book, a reading book, and an English book. Clearly, Mom had decided what to do about school.

"I know I'm not a proper teacher," she announced with a determined expression on her face. "But you shouldn't get behind in school, so this is better than nothing." She pointed at the stapled pages. "That packet has lessons for the week. Follow the instructions. If you have any questions, come ask me. Right?"

"Okay." I nodded slowly. Was I supposed to teach myself? She said I could ask if I had questions, but it seemed she wouldn't explain the lessons first. I wasn't a teacher either. I was only in second grade. Didn't I need a teacher to explain the assignment? How was I going to do this?

I should have known this was coming. Back on Prince of Wales Island (also known as Muralug Island), a lonely English-speaking woman confided that her young sons used correspondence lessons. Some terrible disease ran rampant amongst the islanders, so she feared sending her boys to school. She loved the lessons, and said they were easy to use. Her older son, who was my age, excelled on recent tests, though he had done poorly the year before in a regular mainland school.

With a nod, Mom turned back to work in the galley cleaning the breakfast dishes. Apparently, I would have to sit here until I finished the day's lessons. With a sigh, I picked up the packet and started reading. Under the heading "Monday," assignments for different subjects were listed.

I opened the social studies book and flipped through it curiously, skimming over pages on Aborigines, street signs, and the Flying Doctor service that brought ambulance planes to people in distress in the far reaches of Australia's outback. A picture of Aborigines, the native people of Australia, wearing next to nothing and eating grubs, worm-like creatures, was disgusting but fascinating at the same time.

After a glance at the packet, I flipped to the assigned pages and read about world explorers such as Captain Cook who sailed the world hundreds of years earlier. I examined a map in the book and compared the explorers' routes with our journey so far. Although we'd traveled more than 1,500 miles, the distance seemed tiny on the world map. My face reddened as I remembered asking Mom earlier if we were almost to Grandma's house in America. No wonder she smiled when telling me that we hadn't even reached Indonesia yet.

I quickly finished the spelling and writing lessons from the English book.

Then I read a story from the reading book. A mean boy woke up one topsy-turvy morning to find the dogs treating him as badly as he used to treat them. In the end, the boy changed for the better. I liked happy endings.

I learned to read by age four from a combination of simple phonics lessons from Mom and the new American television show "Sesame Street," and from watching Mom's finger pointing at words as she read stories aloud. Ever since, I'd loved reading. If reading were the largest part of these lessons, teaching myself wouldn't be so hard.

Next came the math assignment. I looked at the pile of books. I carefully picked up each book and set it aside, to make sure it wasn't hidden in the pile, but there was no math book.

"Mom?" I called.

"Yes, Cheryl?" She grabbed a dishtowel and dried her hands, before stepping over to the table.

"What am I supposed to do for math? I can't find the book. How can I do the assignment without the book?" I asked.

"Oh, just skip the math part. We didn't buy a math book. Your dad thought it unnecessary. He'll teach you math when he has time."

He thought the math book was unnecessary? How could a math book be unnecessary? I shrugged my shoulders and figured this must be a joke. Dad liked to tease, but it was odd for Mom to join in. At least I didn't have to do math right now.

Mom looked through one of the oval portholes. "Hmm, plenty of time to do laundry before lunch." She gathered a metal bucket full of dirty cloth diapers, some detergent, and a wooden-framed scrub board with slanted metal slats down its center. "I'll be on deck if you need help." She climbed the few steps to the cockpit outside.

I looked at the stapled pages and then at my work, one more time, just to be sure. It was true.

"Hey, Mom," I yelled as I ran to the deck.

"What is it?" She set down the bucket of seawater she'd just pulled out of the ocean. Setting the washboard in the bucket at an angle, she stood, looking at me expectantly.

"I finished all of Monday's lessons—except math, anyway," I told her excitedly. "Can I go play?"

"As long as you did them properly." She sprinkled some detergent on a dirty diaper and bending down, she scraped it against the scrub board repeatedly. The saltwater wasn't sudsy, but the diaper was soon much cleaner. Mom rinsed it in another bucket of seawater, and hung it on one of the many ropes on deck to dry as much as possible.

Doing lessons on my own wasn't so bad after all. I finished long before lunch, and I could ask questions without worry. I didn't have to wait quietly while the teacher explained the lessons again and again for other students and could go play as soon as I was done.

"Want to play blocks?" Jolene asked after breakfast, a few days later. A hopeful smile hovered on her face.

"I can't!" I huffed. "You know I have to do my lessons first. You asked the same thing yesterday morning."

She asked the same question that day before that, as well. I wanted to play right after breakfast, too. She was lucky. She wasn't required to be in school yet, so she could do whatever she wanted while I had to finish the day's lessons before I could have fun.

"I wish you were done already." Jolene pouted, smacking a few colorful plastic blocks around. In the limited space onboard, we only had a few toys. Our blocks, similar to LEGO™ bricks, were our favorite playthings since we could create so many different toys with them.

"I wish I was done, too." I sighed. "If only I didn't have to do lessons every morning. If only I could skip some days."

I jolted upright. It might work. It just might work. Mom would give me a new packet of lessons each Monday. She probably wouldn't mind if I . . . Yes, it just might work. A smile spread over my face.

On Monday, I put my plan into action and started my lessons, as usual, right after breakfast, but when I finished, I started on Tuesday's lessons.

When Mom set out food for lunch, she looked puzzled. "Aren't you done yet?"

"No, not yet," I said cheerfully.

"Well, clear off the table for now. You'll have to finish up after we eat." She cocked her head and stared at me for a moment.

After lunch, I went back to work. Finally, in the early afternoon, I set my pencil down. With a big grin, I handed Mom a fistful of papers. Mom picked up a pencil and started to check my work. I waited for her to finish.

"Huh? You did the lessons for tomorrow, too?" she asked a few minutes later.

I nodded.

She turned to the next page. "You did Wednesday's lessons, too?" She quickly flipped through the rest. "Well, no wonder you took so long. You did the whole week's lessons!"

"Um-hum," I said as I stowed my books away. Then I bit my lip as I looked at her. "It's okay; isn't it?" I doubted now whether my plan had worked.

"Well . . . I suppose so. If it's done properly, I don't mind if you finish early," she said softly. After she graded the final page, she smiled. "Looks good. You may go play."

Yes! My plan worked. From now on, I would spend Mondays doing lessons. In less time than one Australian school day, I could finish a week's worth of work. Then I had the rest of the week to enjoy without schoolwork. I controlled my own schedule—except for math lessons, since Dad controlled those. Without a math book, how hard could they be anyway?

7. A Slithering Island

As I sat on the deck beside Jolene, some water in the distance caught my eye. I leaned forward, squinting as I tried to figure out why it glimmered and moved in an unusual way.

"Ewww!" I shrieked, jumping back. I couldn't believe it.

"Do you see that?" I yelped at Jolene and pointed to the strange area.

"What is it?" She shaded her eyes with one hand and cocked her head to one side. "Why's the water acting funny like that? It's shiny and wiggly."

"That's what I wondered, but look again. It's not the water." Shaking my head in disbelief, I slowly backed away from the edge of the deck. I took one backward step and then another, trying to distance myself from the water.

"Dad! Dad! Look!" Jolene must have figured it out, too.

"What is it, girls?" Dad hollered from his perch on the aft cabin. The breeze ruffled his dark wavy hair. With one leg crossed over the other, he sat holding the tiller with one hand and a cigarette in the other. Thankfully, the breeze blew the smoke away from us as the stench made me cough and feel nauseous even when I had my sea legs. Whenever conditions were favorable, Dad preferred steering with the carved wooden lever instead of the wheel. He could relax more at the tiller.

He squinted in the direction we pointed.

"Well, I'll be," he said calmly. "Sea snakes. Didn't realize they swarm like that."

Hundreds of long, wriggling sea snakes slipped and slid over each other as they floated along. They slithered about, moving through the water the way their land cousins move across the ground. Swirling, twisting over and under each other, with the sun glinting off their backs, the snakes seemed to ignore us.

I moved back nervously, wondering if they could slither up the side of the hull. There were so many of them, and I wasn't sure what they'd do if they came aboard.

"Can I have one?" Jolene asked with an anxious smile. She squatted down near the railing along the deck's edge, trying to get a closer look.

In Australia, Jolene collected earthworms as pets, but some Aussie worms were quite large, and she often confused worms and snakes. Once she chased a brown snake, thinking it was a worm. She had a jar full of leaves to put it in, so she could admire it up close and keep it for a day or so as a pet. She chased it across the backyard and finally cornered it. Just as she reached her hand out toward it, our family cat bolted across the ground and pounced on the reptile. Snarling and hissing, the cat clawed ferociously, biting the back of the snake's neck as Jolene cried to the cat, pleading with it to leave her new pet alone. The snake fought back, whipping about wildly and sinking its fangs into the howling cat. Mom dashed outside, summoned by the ruckus. She grabbed Jolene around the waist and retreated to the house, ordering me inside immediately, too.

That cat gave her life to save my little sister, but Jolene had been too young to understand why the cat attacked her new pet. She just wanted a worm to love. She didn't understand that some snakes are venomous.

Even now, she looked wistfully at these snakes. If she could have reached down to the surface of the water, she would have picked one up.

"No," Dad said firmly. "No pet snakes. Especially those. Sea snakes are some of the deadliest snakes. Not creatures to play with."

I nodded my head. I knew I didn't like the look of them.

"Um . . . Are they . . ." I trembled slightly as I hopped on the cabin top, farther away from them. "Will they climb up here?"

"Oh, don't worry, Pumpkin." Dad reassured me. "They can't scale a moving boat. We'll be past them soon enough," he promised, though he continued to stare at them.

Jolene gazed longingly at the serpents, while I eased my way down below where I stood on a berth and watched them through the glass porthole, just to be on the safe side. I breathed a huge sigh of relief when the serpents finally disappeared from view.

8. Pierre-Paul Strikes Again

"Juice, Mommy, juice."

I couldn't see Pierre-Paul, since he was in the bedroom he shared with his parents, but I clearly heard his voice from where I sat in the galley playing with Jolene.

"Disgusting," I muttered, rolling my eyes as Marie hustled out of their room. In the galley, she vigorously pumped water into a cup and then hurried back to their room.

Leaning closer to Jolene, I whispered, "Did you notice he never says "please" or "thank you"?"

Jolene nodded. "He's rude and nasty." She'd not forgiven him for throwing her doll overboard, but who could blame her since he'd thrown several other toys over since then?

"'Juice, Mommy, juice," I sneered, copying his annoying tone of voice. "He never asks in a nice voice. Always orders them around."

Whenever he demanded something, his mother ran to fulfill his order, no matter what she was doing. I might only be six-and-a-half years old, but I knew that wasn't the way to teach a child to be a nice person, and I didn't understand why she put up with it.

He must have finished his drink because his mother returned the cup, and he ambled out of their room into the galley.

I took a deep breath and decided to be friendly. "Want to play with us?" I pointed to our latest plastic-block creation. "We're taking the house apart. Want to make something new with us?"

He nodded and took a couple of blocks, but instead of sitting down to play, he ran and stopped in the tiny hallway, just outside his family's bedroom.

"Hey, what're you doing?" I craned my neck to see, but the unlit hallway was too dim.

He crouched in a corner and said nothing, but I heard scraping and scratching noises. A minute later, he stood up and sauntered over with a look in his eye that spelled trouble.

"Where are they?" I asked as I looked for the blocks he'd taken. I saw no pockets in his clothing, and his hands hung by his side, empty. There weren't any strange bulges in his clothes. Where could our blocks be? They were our toys and not his, after all.

Silently, he smirked and pointed at the floor.

I walked over and studied the hallway floorboards, but saw nothing. I felt around, in case I missed them in the low light. Then I said, "Huh? I don't see them. Where are they?"

"In the floor," he sneered, raising his eyebrows. His smirk grew bigger.

I looked at Jolene, but she shrugged. She had no idea what he meant, either.

"Well, don't lose our blocks. We can't get any more." Then I went back and took the rest of the house apart. Jolene and I decided our next creation would be a boat.

Pierre-Paul stared at us for a while, looking pleased with himself and rather triumphant.

Apparently, he didn't understand that we couldn't go to a store and buy replacements, or maybe he didn't care, because day after day more of our blocks vanished without a trace.

"What are you doing?" I shrieked when I finally glimpsed him in the act.

He beamed a wicked-looking grin at me, and then darted back into the safety of his bedroom.

"What did he do?" Jolene walked to the tiny dark spot where he always took our things.

"Come here and look." I beckoned. "See right there?" I pointed to a spot where the floorboards met the bulkhead.

"Yeah." Jolene raised her eyebrows at me and shrugged. "But I don't see anything. Just the floor and the wall. Do you know where the blocks are?" She turned this way and that, with a puzzled expression on her face.

"Not over there. Look right here!" I got down on my knees and pointed repeatedly at a slight crack between two floorboards. "He's been stuffing our blocks in there. They're in the bilge!"

Whenever water splashed onboard, it eventually drained into the bilge, the area under the floorboards. Dirt from people's shoes, spilled food or drink, and anything else that fell into the floor's crevices, landed in the bilge, too. The bilge, with its filthy water, was the boat's sewer. Eventually its nasty, dirty water was pumped overboard, back into the sea, so the boat didn't fill up and sink. The blocks he'd somehow squeezed through that tiny crevice were gone forever.

Getting up, I went in search of Marie. I told her what Pierre-Paul had been doing, but she shrugged her shoulders as if to say, "What can I do?"

I thought for a minute. What could she do? She was a grown-up; wasn't she? She was his mother; wasn't she? Couldn't she take charge, punish him, and make him sorry enough that he wouldn't do it again? But since she let him order her around all the time, maybe she didn't know how to be a grown-up.

My mom never ignored a problem like that. She listened and came up with a solution. She fixed problems when she could and punished naughty children when needed, so I went to explain the situation to her.

Mom asked me to show her the crack. After looking at it, she told me to wait there.

When she returned, she said, "I spoke to Marie. She said she'd handle it. He's her son, so she should be the one to take care of it."

I sighed. Marie hadn't done anything when I told her about the problem. She never disciplined Pierre-Paul as far as I could see. She never even said "no" to him. Instead, she treated him as if he were in charge. I didn't expect her to do anything more now.

The next day, Pierre-Paul grabbed two slanted red blocks, ones we usually used as roof pieces, and ran off. I tried to grab him, but he was too quick. Two more blocks were gone forever.

He tossed more toys over the side, too, as he'd done earlier with Jolene's doll. If he kept this up, we'd soon have no playthings left. All of our toys would be at the bottom of the ocean.

Then one day, something happened that was worse, much worse.

"Mom, Pear-Paw took my Bible. I saw him and he won't give it back," I whined. I was so tired of his annoying behavior.

Mom sighed and shrugged her shoulders. "Cheryl, his mom needs to handle this because she's his mom." Mom was not going to interfere.

"Can't you get it back? Please? Please?" I looked up at her, my eyes brimming with tears that threatened to fall.

The Bible had been a gift, and a Bible was a special book. It was a book to be treated with respect, but Pierre-Paul had no respect for anyone or anything—not even a Bible. How he did it, I couldn't figure out, but shining a torch over the crevice, I saw a telltale corner of the Bible. Somehow, he shoved it into the bilge. Completely soaked with filthy, disgusting bilge water, the Bible was ruined.

Something needed to be done about Pierre-Paul. Soon.

9. MATH LESSONS

One afternoon, about a week out of Darwin, Claude sat at the tiller, taking his four-hour shift on watch. The ocean was calm. The breeze was light on this beautiful day.

Dad called for me to come down to the galley, saying, "Time to start math lessons."

I shrugged my shoulders at Jolene and left her on the deck where we'd been playing together. I'd been expecting this for several days.

"Why is the book unnecessary?" I asked when I sat down on a berth.

In one hand, he held a sheet of paper that he slapped against his other hand. "Modern rubbish!" He spat the words out. "Teaching math by playing with silly pieces of wood. What a waste of time!"

"You mean the rods we used in school?" Colorful wooden Cuisenaire rods were the latest method of teaching basic math skills. "They're fun."

"Well, I'm not about to waste my hard-earned money on that nonsense. The old methods were good enough for me, and they'll do for you, too." Dad bought the other lesson materials from the Australian government's school system. We used them differently than families in Australia's never-never, hundreds of miles from the nearest school, usually did. We didn't mail each week's lessons back for grading, and wait to get the next week's lessons in the mail; instead, my parents graded and kept my work, so they could change the lessons if they wanted.

"I've written the two times tables." He handed me a sheet of notebook paper with a column of math problems on it. "Copy these one hundred times each. When you're done, let me know. Any questions?"

I stood for a minute, considering what I'd heard. Did he really say what I thought he'd said? Surely, I must have misunderstood.

Finally, I spoke up. "One hundred times? Each?" I gulped.

"You heard me. Copy them properly." Satisfied that I understood, he turned and headed to the cockpit.

He joked and teased a lot, but his voice sounded serious this time. I didn't want to get into trouble, so, shaking my head in disbelief, I sat and picked up a pencil.

I wrote "2 x 0 = 0" at the top of a piece of paper. Three times, I wrote it across the page. Then I did the same on the next line. When I'd filled every line, I stopped and counted seventy-five problems. I wasn't done yet! And this was just the first problem!

My hand started to ache. I tried to set the pencil on the table, but my hand was so stiff, it took a few moments to open my fingers and let go of the pencil. I flexed my fingers a few times and then shook my hand, trying to loosen the muscles. Then, I went back to work. None of my schoolteachers had ever given me an assignment this long—not even the crazy teacher in Hervey Bay—but I knew better than to complain.

"Two times ten equals twenty," I said to myself later in the day as I copied the final problem. I stopped and stretched my hand before counting, to double check that I was truly done.

"One hundred. At last," I muttered. Stretching my arms, I moved my shoulders up and down a few times, and rotated my head back and forth, easing my tired muscles. Then I grabbed the pile of papers and went to search for Dad.

I found him sitting on the main cabin. Beside him lay a rope with several inches unraveled on one end. He held another rope and busily frayed its end. Handing the stack to him, I announced, "I'm done."

Dad slowly flipped through the papers. I was fairly certain he counted the problems. "You can go," was all he said when he finished. He returned to his chore, twisting the frayed ends together to merge two ropes into a longer one.

That was all there was to the math lesson? All that time and energy spent writing so much, and that was all he had to say? It didn't seem right.

However, the math lesson wasn't over.

An hour or so later, his voice startled me. "Time for a quiz."

I'd been lying on the deck, lazily watching the ocean and enjoying the soft breeze, since down below, even with the hatches open, the air felt stuffy at times. I sat up and looked at Dad, as he barked, "Two times six." He snapped his fingers almost immediately after uttering the last word.

"Um . . . Two times six is . . . twelve," I answered.

"Wrong!"

Hmm? I was pretty sure two times six was twelve. After all, six plus six was twelve, and aren't they really the same problem? So why did he say I was wrong?

"If you repeat the problem, you're stalling for time. Give me the correct answer before I snap my fingers or it's wrong, and you'll copy it another hundred times."

Oh. That explained that. My hand was still sore from all that writing. I didn't want to copy any of them another hundred times. That was just too much, but I wasn't about to say that aloud. Dad had a fiery temper at times. His yelling and slamming things scared me. Besides, he was likely to give spankings when mad, so I'd rather avoid making him mad.

The math lessons never changed. At random times, Dad produced a new list of problems to copy a hundred times each.

Remembering his quiz, I said each problem aloud as I copied it, hoping to fix it in my memory, so I wouldn't have to copy it again later.

Dad's tests included problems from previous lessons, too, so I tried not to forget any lest I have to copy them another hundred times. The math lessons weren't exciting, but Dad explained that the exciting stuff came later and that math was a tool to help do great things.

I knew that. Every day, as noon approached, Dad took out a black, triangular sextant and a chronometer. The chronometer was a very expensive pocket watch that kept exceedingly accurate time. Actually, he'd saved money buying a slightly broken chronometer. Despite its missing hour hand, Dad used it to determine the precise moment noon struck. He looked through the sextant's eyepiece and moved the curved bottom of the instrument until the horizon's edge appeared in the viewfinder and the sun's reflection in the sextant's mirror. Then he wrote down the numbers indicated on the bottom of the tool.

Inside the main cabin, just off of the galley in a tiny closet-sized room that held his navigation desk, Dad pulled out a thick book of numbers. Using these trigonometric tables, he converted his measurements to new numbers. Somehow, by shifting the middle section of his slide rule, he calculated our longitude and latitude. Surrounded by water, with no signs or landmarks in sight, he used math to find our exact location on a map.

"Learning to use a hammer properly is boring, but you have to master the hammer before you can become a carpenter and build great things.

It's the same with math; you've got to master the basic facts first," he explained.

It made sense to me, so I didn't complain about the tedious math lessons. Especially since his lessons were infrequent. They came whenever he thought about it. A few days, or even a week or more, passed between his math lessons.

10. South of Roti and Timor Islands, Indonesia

"Looks like a great surfing beach," Dad said as we sailed close to Roti, an Indonesian island. "It's got to be one of the best in the world. I'll bet the surfies don't know about it." Large waves rolled onto the beach, as we passed by close enough to see people leaving their huts but not a single surfboard.

"Oh, let's stop here. I'd love to sun on the beach or go shopping." Marie, like me, had been seasick the first three days out of Darwin, but now she had her sea legs and was ready for action of some sort.

"Not a chance. Put up every sail," Dad ordered. "I want out of here fast, before the locals come meet us."

"What's the hurry?" Bill asked. "Let's anchor and go sightseeing. I signed on to see the world, to explore new lands, and meet new people. That island looks like a great place to begin."

"Trust me; you don't want to explore this island. Some of the people might be nice, but pirates are a problem around here. They'll steal everything, maybe even the boat. Then how will you see the world?"

Bill looked longingly at the island for a moment. Then he shook his head and hurried to help Claude and Marie hoist more sails.

We sped between Roti and another tiny island, through the Timor Sea, on our way to Christmas Island. Since leaving Darwin a week earlier, we'd averaged about fifty miles a day, but now, under full sail, we ran 128 miles in a single day as we raced away from the pirate-infested waters.

A couple of days later, Claude sat at the tiller after supper, taking his turn at watch. The rest of us lounged around the cockpit, chatting and enjoying the gorgeous sunset.

"Hey, did you see that?" Claude asked, excitedly. "Hey, there it goes again!" He pointed, and we turned, trying to spot whatever it was.

"Look, over there!" he called a third time.

"Wow! What is it?"

"I saw it this time."

"Me, too."

Everyone talked at once, pointing toward the horizon where a bright light plummeted through the fading sunlight, like a distant firework explosion.

"Is it a flare?" Mom asked. "Maybe someone's in trouble?" If it were a signal for help, we'd have to change course and go assist. That was the law of the sea.

Dad stood up. He set his cup down and shooed everyone off one of the cockpit benches. Lifting its top, he reached in the storage compartment and grabbed his binoculars. Then, he studied the area where the lights had been. Another flashed and then another.

"Well? What is it?" someone asked nervously.

Dad snorted as he let the binoculars drop so they hung around his neck. Reaching over, he mussed my hair. "Nothing to worry about," he reassured everyone. "Only lightning. Not flares. Not close enough for us to worry about."

More and more lightning bolts burst through the sky along the horizon.

Mom leaned back against the bench. "Looks like a fireworks display to me." She sighed. "It's beautiful."

Everyone murmured agreement and relaxed again, enjoying the brilliant light show provided by nature.

"Red sky at night, sailor's delight. Red sky in morning, sailors take warning," Dad quoted in a worried voice a couple of days later. As we finished our breakfast, he described the gorgeous rose-colored sunrise he witnessed during his watch.

When breakfast was over, I went on deck. The day seemed bright and clear without a cloud in sight. The breeze was steady. The weather seemed much like the weather of the previous beautiful day. Why was Dad worried? The proverb must be just a silly superstition.

However, as afternoon came, the waves grew larger, and the wind picked up speed.

"Girls, go down below," Mom advised, as Dad sent the crew scurrying to close the hatches and secure everything on deck.

I climbed on a lower berth in the galley and stood, peering through the high porthole at the sea around us. "Hmm, that's strange," I muttered to myself.

Jolene scrambled up beside me, but even on her tiptoes, she was too short to see more than the sky overhead.

"Here, I'll lift you up," I offered, hoisting her for a few moments.

"I saw the ocean, the ocean with lots of waves in it. What's strange about that?"

"You didn't notice anything wrong with the waves?" I puzzled over what I'd seen, trying to make sense of it.

"Nope. Just looked like waves, bigger than usual waves." She shrugged.

"Here, look again. Look at the direction they're going." I grunted as I lifted her once more.

"Hey, they're going two directions," she said, as I dropped her again.

"Right. I wonder why?" I watched the waves grow higher and higher.

This was our first storm at sea! A little scary, but it was exciting, too, after days of easy sailing. Instead of the usual smooth gentle rocking motion, the boat now reeled forcefully. Instead of waves gently shushing past the hull, some crashed over the deck. As the wind's speed grew, so did its noise level.

The grownups, one at a time, came down below and grabbed a set of bright yellow, foul-weather gear. They pulled the waterproof pants over their shorts, and then donned the hooded jackets over their t-shirts. Protected from flying water and the brisk chilly wind, they scurried back on deck, letting water whip through the cabin as they exited.

"Jackie!" A panicked expression flooded Mom's face as she ran to Pierre-Paul's family's bedroom, which wasn't as private as they would have liked, since it was the most secure place to stow the baby's basket. She returned in a moment, looking calmer. "We were drenched here in the galley, but she's sleeping like a baby, dry and snug. Her blankets aren't even damp."

Outside, I heard Dad yell, "Lower the jib!"

Claude and Marie dropped the sail and secured it in place more efficiently and gracefully than a week ago. They worked harder than our previous crews and were becoming better sailors day by day, though I wished they would control their son who regularly destroyed our things.

"Belay the mizzen sheet!" Dad ordered as a rope on the shorter aft mast came loose and whipped wildly in the air.

Marie scrambled to secure the line.

Rrrrip. The pressure of a strong gust tore a sail.

"Trim that sail!" Dad yelled, pulling his rain hood forward. The wind pushed our ketch too hard, too quickly. The sails couldn't handle it. We needed to reef, or even lower completely, some sails and slow the ship down.

Waves crashed. Water sprayed all about. The ship rocked faster. The crew ran madly, leaning against the wind at times. Storm clouds blotted out much of the sunlight.

"The bilge pump! Marie! Man the bilge pump," ordered Dad.

Waves crashed over the deck, constantly dumping water across the *Berenice*. If she filled with water, she would surely sink. Marie rushed to the bilge pump. She pulled the metal handle up with both hands, and then, grunting and grimacing, she pushed it down. Repeatedly she pumped, up and down, up and down, sending the water back into the sea, where it belonged. The sea never stopped, so Marie pumped, up and down, up and down, over and over again, even when her arms trembled under the strain.

In the galley, Mom made coffee and damper, staples in our diet. Donning her foul weather gear, she carried a steaming cup and a piece of warm pan-fried bread up the ladder. As she opened the door, the wind tore it out of her hand, slamming and banging it against the side of the cabin, until she grabbed it and bolted it shut again. Clinging to the cabin, she traversed the couple of feet to the wheel, and shoved at Dad the cup with its mixture of coffee and storm water and the drenched Australian bread. Competing with the sounds of the storm, she yelled, urging him to eat something to keep up his strength.

Bolting the door shut again when she returned, she took off her rain gear and set to work cleaning up. Everything in the galley was soaked from the water that whipped into the cabin when the door was open. Try as she might, it was impossible to dry out the drenched cabin.

Bill relieved Marie at the bilge pump. His strong arms moved up and down, up and down, rather quickly at first, but soon, he dragged and his arms shook with the effort. Claude relieved him until he, too, was exhausted, and Marie took over the job once more.

"Want a story?" I asked Jolene and Pierre-Paul, trying to distract them—and myself, too—from the nasty weather outside. The adults didn't let us help fight the storm, so we were left to ourselves, with little to do besides listen, watch, and worry.

"It's too dark in here to read," Jolene whined, as she sat beside me on the lower berth.

"Dark," agreed Pierre-Paul.

We children weren't allowed to use a kerosene lantern, especially during a storm when the weather might knock it over and start a fire. Besides, fuel was too precious to waste on making ourselves comfortable, and the electric lights weren't an option, since the engine wasn't functioning. Again.

"That's okay," I said, as Pierre-Paul edged closer. "I know lots of stories. I can make up something, if you want . . ."

"All right." Jolene nodded her head and shifted into a comfortable position at my side.

Pierre-Paul didn't say anything but plopped down near my feet.

"Well, let me see," I said, thinking aloud. "I know. Once upon a time, there was a house with three bears in it."

In my mixed-up fairy tale, Cinderella came to the three bears' house looking for her lost glass slipper. The Big Bad Wolf tried to blow the house down until Prince Charming stopped him with some magic beans. Jolene and Pierre-Paul laughed at the crazy, unexpected parts of the story and at my silly voices and sound effects.

At the end of the story, I smiled. No one complained about the storm, the darkness, or the dampness during the story. I hadn't thought about them either, since I concentrated on the story. While the grownups had plenty to deal with, I kept the children from bothering them, so I had helped, in my own small way.

Eating supper that night was a challenge. Mom raised the folding table leaves into place. Then we sat, took the plates of food she distributed, and bowed our heads for the blessing. The table was firmly bolted to the floor, so it swayed and lurched with the *Berenice* as the wind and waves knocked her about, and everything slid off the table unless held securely, so eating was a juggling act. I drank most of my water first and then wedged the cup between my knees. One hand held my plate steady, while I held the fork with the other. Any sudden jerk from a strong gust of wind sent bits of food flying, so more cleaning than usual was required after the meal, but we managed to eat most of it.

Then we went to bed. Usually Dad and the crew took turns on watch throughout the night, so someone steered at all times, yet everyone got a chance to sleep for several hours at a time—or that was how it should work.

"What's wrong?" Claude asked when he trudged back to his bedroom after his four-hour stint on watch and found his wife lying stiffly with eyes wide open. "Why're you still awake?"

"I can't. I just can't. The boat's going so fast, too fast." She stifled a sob. "I'm afraid I won't wake up again."

Claude tried to comfort her, but Marie lay wide-awake all night long.

Dad didn't get any sleep either. He wouldn't give up the helm while the storm raged, except for a rare, brief trip to the head. When Bill came up to relieve him, Dad refused to go to bed since he was the most experienced sailor. Besides, as captain of the ship, he was duty-bound to protect the ship and all aboard through danger. Bill stayed on deck to help, but Dad steered for another four hours. When Claude relieved Bill, at the end of the watch, Dad continued at the wheel with Claude's help. All night long, Dad steered.

When I awoke the next morning, something felt different. I sat up and looked around. Nothing inside appeared different from yesterday. What was the matter then? Suddenly I realized there was stillness and silence. During the storm, the wind howled, the waves crashed into the sea and slammed against the *Berenice*, and the rain thrummed on the exterior of the boat, but those noises were gone now. Now, the faint shushing of water streaming past the hull, the creaking of rigging, and the murmur of voices talking elsewhere on the boat were audible once more. The boat swayed gently, steadily, rather than rocking savagely. The storm was over. We'd survived our first storm at sea.

Dad sat cross-legged on the deck with a pile of white canvas spread across his lap and all around him. The dark circles under his eyes were more pronounced than usual, but he sang a silly song about Barnacle Bill as he hunched over the sail. On one hand, he wore a thick leather protector. This fingerless backless glove prevented the large curved needle from piercing his palm as he pushed the needle and extra strong thread through the dense canvas. Making a stitch on one side of the rip and then the other, he sewed back and forth, darning the ripped sail as Mom might darn a torn sock.

We pulled through with little damage. Some sails had been ripped by the winds, but that was expected in hard weather. The spinnaker pole, which could be used to rig an extra sail in the front of the boat, was broken, but the masts weren't damaged. The hull was sound. No leaks had sprung. Overall, the *Berenice* had proven she was tough. She took on a tempest without breaking apart. Everyone onboard smiled. We were proud that we'd passed the test, though we didn't want to face another storm anytime soon.

Little did we know this storm was tiny, miniscule, in comparison to the storms we would encounter later. It was nothing in comparison to the big one that was coming soon, nothing compared to a cyclone.

11. Christmas Island

"Land! Land!" Dad whooped from the top of the mast. He sat on the spreader, the cross piece near the top of the mast, legs dangling down, one hand shielding his eyes from the sun and the other holding tightly to the mast. Despite his fear of heights, he climbed the mast when necessary to get a better view.

Bill sat at the tiller steering, while the rest of us lingered below over breakfast. There was coffee for the grown-ups, water for the kids, and Mom's freshly cooked damper topped with Golden Syrup for everyone. Hearing Dad's yell, Mom hammered the lid down on the tin, closing it like a can of paint, and everyone scrambled for the companionway, competing to be first up the ladder.

Though it seemed like ages since we'd seen land, it had only been a couple of weeks. At first, we saw nothing but water. Did Dad really spot land? Perhaps he suffered from wishful thinking and imagined it? Yet, eventually, off in the distance, barely visible, a vague misty haze appeared on the horizon. Slowly it took form, gradually becoming an island.

After gazing at it for a few minutes, we returned below to finish our breakfast and hurriedly prepare for our arrival. I finished letters to Nanny and Grandma Bernice, my grandmothers in far-off Missouri, telling of our adventures so far. Mom added her letters to mine. We'd mail them at the local post office when we checked to see if any mail waited for us.

We'd told relatives our next destination. They could write us there, listing our street address as "general delivery." The post office would hold letters or packages behind the counter until we came and asked for them. Of course, if we didn't stop as planned, the mail would never reach us, but in the days before internet, cell phones, and other easy methods of international communication, general delivery mail gave us a relatively inexpensive way to keep in touch throughout our journey.

Claude and Marie hustled to their bedroom to dig out their wallets. After more than two weeks at sea where money was useless, it took a while to find them. They planned to go sightseeing.

Mom grabbed a pencil and paper. She opened cabinet doors and peeked in the storage areas under the berths making notes about things she'd like to pick up at the local market. Fresh fruits and vegetables would be nice. Eggs and real milk would be a treat. Perhaps she'd even buy enough fresh meat for a meal or two. Since we didn't have refrigeration—not really, not on an ongoing basis, since the fickle engine's battery powered the fridge, and both consumed precious fuel—we could buy only limited quantities of meat, milk, and eggs.

On deck, I watched as Christmas Island grew larger and larger. Seeming to grow from nothing into a full-sized island right before my very eyes, I felt as though I watched the creation story in progress. I felt a tingle of excitement down my spine as I thought about the new adventure about to unfold.

"Mom, what's that boat with the funny sails," I asked that afternoon as we motored into Flying Fish Cove, the only harbor on an island whose coastline was mostly high, rocky cliffs.

"Which boat?" she asked, as she sorted through a pile of clothing, looking for respectable clothes. At sea, we often wore the same clothes repeatedly, mostly swimming togs or cotton shorts and t-shirts, since there weren't any neighbors to see us and drying wet laundry was almost impossible. On shore, we dressed nicer and even wore shoes.

"That boat, the one with the almost square-shaped sails that have sticks running across them." I pointed at a wooden boat whose sails resembled misshapen pieces of lined paper.

"Oh, that? It's a junk. A Chinese-style boat." She turned around and went back to her preparations.

I gazed out the porthole at the junk. "Hey, Jolene, look at the funny hat." I pointed at a beige straw hat.

Climbing onto a bunk, she stretched, trying to see through the small, high window. I gave her a boost, and she said, "It's nice. I'd like a hat like that. It looks like an upside-down ice-cream cone." She giggled. "What's that woman doing, anyway?"

A sudden noise came from within the cabin. We jerked around and scrambled to grab the few toys that were out. Quickly, we put them where

Pierre-Paul couldn't grab them. We never left anything in his path, if possible, anymore.

Once our things were safe, we went back to the porthole. People on a boat near us sat cross-legged, with massive grayish-beige piles in front of them. Were they piles of rope, maybe? As we continued watching, they picked up bits of knotted rope. Their hands moved this way and that. Ah, they were repairing fishing nets.

On the beach, a woman poured something from a bowl onto the ground. Over and over, she poured little puddles. What was she doing? What was that stuff? Behind her, curled pastel-colored things, slightly smaller than her palm, lay neatly in rows.

Once the *Berenice* docked, and harbor officials reviewed our passports and health certificates, we hurried ashore, glad to set foot on dry ground again. Dad took care of ship's business. Our crew went sightseeing, and Mom took us girls for a stroll along the beach. Jolene and I raced along the beach, happy to have room to run after being cooped up for so long.

"Let's see what she's doing," I yelled to Jolene, pointing to the woman we watched earlier.

"Slow down and don't bother her," Mom warned as she lagged behind, struggling to push the baby's stroller through the sand.

Up close, I saw the tiny puddles—about the size of an apple—shrinking and curling. As they dried in the sun, brilliant pastel colors emerged. Another woman gathered the dried pink, orange, green, and yellow bits into a basket. She looked over at me and smiled. She held one in her hand, turning it this way and that. Then she popped it in her mouth and bit off a piece. She smiled again and held one out towards us.

They looked like fluffy, colorful potato chips or crisps, as Aussies call them, but I'd never heard of sunbaked chips. I'd never seen colorful chips before, either.

When Mom caught up, she spoke with the woman. The chips were made of fish to be sold in the market. Mom paid the woman and took a batch, handing a few to Jolene and me.

Holding mine to the light, I examined one first. Thicker than a potato chip, it was full of air pockets, bubbles. Gingerly, I took a small nibble. Yum, yum. It tasted like a puffy, salty potato chip with just a little something different. Something deliciously different. I wasn't sure how they turned fresh fish into chips, but these were wonderful.

The women bowed and smiled as we savored their creation. Scooting closer, the black-haired women reached out to touch my hair. They stroked it repeatedly. Though they smiled, I felt like an animal in a petting zoo exhibit.

As we continued our walk, other locals approached, reaching for my hair that had been bleached by the sun and salt air until it was pure white. Jolene's strawberry blonde hair was now almost white with a peach undertone and drew similar attention. Apparently, the islanders had never seen such light-colored hair, and they thought stroking it would bring them good luck.

"Carolyn!" Dad waved at us to return to the dock. "There's a gentleman here I'd like you to meet."

A man grinned at us. He looked about Dad's age, in his early thirties. "Don't get many visitors around here. Saw you arrive. I was just telling your husband that I'm here, far from home, managing the mining company. We mine phosphate, the island's biggest resource." He pointed at the ships and mining equipment that filled the harbor.

Dad introduced us properly.

"Nice to meet you," Mom replied.

"It's rather lonely out here. I'm not married, you see, and the natives are nice, but it's not quite the same as back home, if you know what I mean. Anyway, thought you might enjoy being shown around the island."

After a tour of the island, he took us to dinner with several other English-speaking islanders who were anxious to hear news from back home and socialize with someone new.

"Tell you what, why don't you take a look at the company store in the morning? You'll likely find things more to your liking there than the Chinese market, since we ship in stuff directly from Australia for our employees. You'll find supplies you're used to there. I'll let the clerk know you're coming since the store's usually open only to employees. He'll treat you right," our host said at the end of the evening before bidding us goodnight.

The next morning, Mom took us girls with her to the small shop. As the manager predicted, the store was full of familiar items. Vegetables, fruits, boxed foods, canned foods, and more filled the shelves. Racks of clothing and tools sat alongside soft drinks.

"Oh, my!" Mom exclaimed when she picked up an item and saw the price. "My goodness!" she said after looking at yet another price tag. "I can't believe these prices!"

"Ah yes," the clerk agreed. "Ridiculous, aren't they?"

"People pay this much? How do you stay in business?" Mom asked.

"Well, that's the price we pay for bringing items all the way from mainland Australia. Transportation costs are exorbitant, but these things wouldn't be for sale on the island otherwise, so if people want them, they pay."

"I don't know. I planned to stock up on more supplies, but we can afford prices like this." Mom shook her head.

The clerk looked at Jackie in her stroller, and then leaned in closer. "You might want to try the Chinese market instead. The goods won't seem so familiar, but you might find a few things you can buy. They'll still be expensive, since most things have to be shipped over, but they come from China or Singapore, which aren't as far away, so they won't be quite as dear."

Mom thanked him and got directions for the Chinese market.

The next morning, Mom and we three girls trekked to the other market. Here, strange writing—Chinese characters—covered the signs. People spoke in singsong words that I couldn't understand, though I listened carefully and soon tried saying a few of them. Strange odors filled the air. Baskets held a variety of plants. Some may have been spices. Others were clearly fruits or vegetables, but some were a mystery to me. Meat hung outside, with flies buzzing around, at what looked like altars. I'm glad Mom didn't buy any. The smell was so overpowering I couldn't imagine eating it.

Mom bought some inexpensive dishes, including a set of beautiful ceramic bowls with traditional Chinese designs painted on them. The matching soupspoons weren't metal, like the spoons I knew. Instead, these were ceramic, and resembled tiny oval-shaped bowls stretched on one side to form long curved handles. She also bought several sets of chopsticks. Wooden ones with designs painted on them, and other fancier ones made of ivory with beautiful colorful dragons and other designs etched on them.

I'd never seen chopsticks before. A kind, raven-haired man patiently demonstrated how to hold them and pick up food. It looked simple when he did it, but when I held the two sticks in one hand and tried it, nothing stayed between the chopsticks. He gently moved my fingers and showed me how to hold them like a pair of scissors. After a few more tries, I picked up bits of food. Jolene and Mom soon figured them out, too. Smiling and nodding, the gentleman praised us for learning to use them, giving the impression that few English-speaking people bothered to learn.

A petite woman silently watched the lesson. Then she pulled out a piece of cloth with metal rods sewn into it and handed it to Mom, nodding and smiling.

"No, thank you." Mom shook her head, and looked dubiously at whatever the thing was. She waved her hands to show that she didn't want to buy it.

"Take, take," the woman insisted.

"No, thank you."

After much gesturing and halting English, the woman finally conveyed that she was giving a gift. Bowing, she took the cloth and attached the bars to Jackie's stroller. She then pointed at the sun and back at the baby.

"Ah, thank you very much," Mom said, her eyes wide. "An awning, to protect her from the sun. Thank you." She nodded repeatedly, copying the woman's bowing.

Back aboard the *Berenice*, Mom carefully wrapped the dishes and spoons in layers of cloth and stored them amongst soft, rarely used clothing where she hoped they would stay safe if another storm struck. If a storm struck? More likely, when. When another storm struck. We hoped we'd been through the worst storm and the rest of the journey would be easier, but we knew more storms were inevitable.

"Is that all you got?" Dad asked when he popped down into the cabin. "Where's the fresh food?"

Mom grimaced. "I think we have a problem. A big problem," she said. "We've miscalculated. I'm afraid we won't have enough money to make it."

The prices for fresh vegetables, milk, and other items had been extremely high at the local market, too. Christmas Island was more than a hundred miles from Java, one of Singapore's main islands, and even farther from Australia. Anything not grown or made on the island was outrageously expensive—often more than ten or twenty times the price we expected. A huge sum had been spent along the way on engine repairs, too.

"We've got plenty of supplies stored away; haven't we?" Dad asked.

"For now, yes."

"Well, we'll be careful and stretch things out as much as possible. We might have to keep eating tinned food, but we'll make it, somehow."

"I did get a dozen eggs," Mom added. "I met a lovely islander who raises chickens. Wally, you wouldn't believe how much she could have charged for them in the market, but she gave them to me. With eggs, we can have pancakes or cake or . . . Well, there are so many possibilities."

"But the fridge isn't running. Won't they spoil after a day or two?"

"I worried about the same thing, but you won't believe what she told me. She doesn't have a fridge, but doesn't worry about them going bad."

Her secret? Vaseline. Yes, Vaseline. The greasy stuff we sometimes put on the baby's bottom could be spread on an egg. Apparently, this sealed the tiny pores on the egg, so oxygen and microorganisms couldn't invade the egg. The egg would be preserved, like fruit in a can, for a much longer life than usually possible without refrigeration.

Mom was skeptical. Would it actually work? She always refrigerated her eggs. She didn't want to poison the family, but with a gift, she dared to experiment. She tested the idea on a few eggs to see if it worked.

"Blech! Nasty!" I complained. Shuddering, I tried to rub the taste off my tongue.

Jolene spat a bite of eggs on her plate.

"Perhaps there's a way to keep the eggs from tasting like Vaseline?" Dad suggested when even he had trouble swallowing the food.

Perhaps Mom asked the woman for further explanation, or maybe she figured it out on her own, but Mom tried again. This time she dipped the fresh eggs briefly, very briefly, into boiling water to close the pores on the eggs. When we smeared Vaseline on the eggs, the greasy stuff stayed on the outside of the eggs, rather than seeping inside.

The next time Mom cooked eggs, they tasted like ordinary chicken eggs. The idea worked. Maybe the salty sea air had something to do with it, too, since salt kills many microorganisms. Whatever the reason, we were able to keep eggs fresh for weeks without refrigeration; none went bad. Now we could enjoy pancakes and other dishes that had previously been impossible far out at sea.

During our five-day stay on Christmas Island, Dad made repairs. Sails that had torn during the storm were sewn. The braces that secured

Bill's berth to the cement hull had come loose and were reattached. The spinnaker pole was mended.

The two masts each had a boom that could hold a sail. The spinnaker pole and jib could be rigged to fly more sails, so having the spinnaker pole fixed meant we could have more sail power, and go faster.

Repairs were usually a necessity when a boat moored in harbor. Sailing put a lot of wear on various parts of a boat, and these repairs were part of the expected maintenance, but one repair was not expected.

"Grrr," Dad muttered as he stormed about. "Piece of junk!" He whacked a spanner, or a monkey wrench, against the engine in frustration. "Money down the tubes! I hate this wretched pile of rubbish!" As he worked in the cramped engine area under the cockpit, he yelled or sometimes muttered.

I didn't get close enough to see exactly what he was doing. I knew better, when he was this upset.

Overhauling the engine cost money. A lot of money. Money he planned to use for supplies. Besides, he'd overhauled it completely, from top to bottom, six times. Six! This engine and the ocean didn't seem to get along, no matter what he, or any other mechanic, did to fix it. Would this repair be any different? Would it last more than a few days?

From Christmas Island, we set sail for the Cocos Islands in the Indian Ocean, about six hundred miles west. The Cocos Islands, which belonged to Australia, would be our last stop in Australian territory. Then we'd head to the Indochina area in southern Asia. From there, we'd sail south, around Africa, and cross the Atlantic Ocean. Going through the Caribbean Islands, we'd journey up to the United States, where we'd visit relatives for a few months. Relatives we hadn't seen in six years—since I was a baby. Afterwards, we'd head down to the Panama Canal and sail through the Americas. Then our yacht would carry us across the Pacific Ocean and back to Australia, back to our home. We'd travel around the world in our ferro-cement boat. At least, that was the plan. Of course, plans often go awry.

The *Berenice* under construction. From "Former Local Resident Plans World Cruise In "Home Built" Yacht." *Trenton Republican-Times*, ca. April 1971. Used with permission.

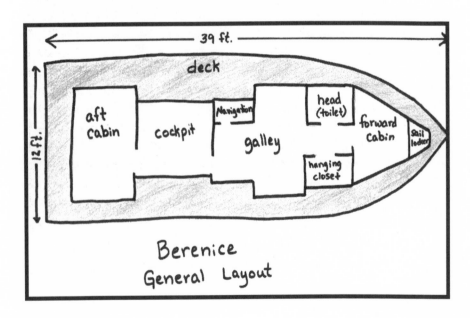

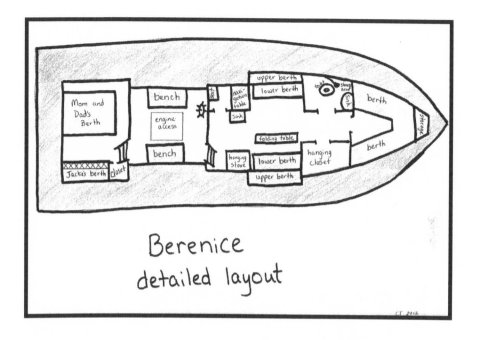

Berenice
detailed layout

Copy of one of the many articles printed in newspapers about our trip. Reprinted from *Trenton Republican-Times,* ca. Aug. 1971. Used with permission.

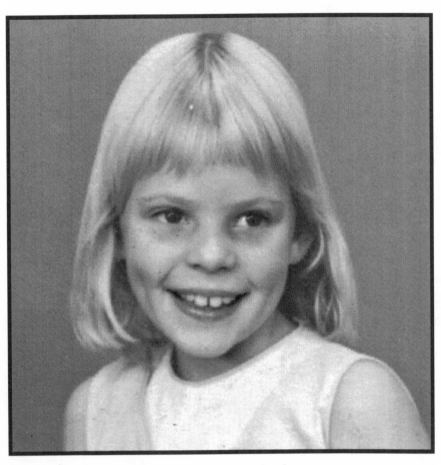

Cheryl in Durban, South Africa.
Standard One (equivalent to third grade). 1972.

Jolene in Durban, South Africa.
Class A (equivalent to first grade). 1972.

Dad, Mom, and Cheryl in their shared passport photo.
Darwin, Australia. 1971.

12. The Never-Ending Storm

Sep. 18, 1971

"Batten down the hatches!" Dad yelled, just a day out of Christmas Island.

The crew raced about, latching hatches shut, stowing away small loose objects, and tying down bigger ones. The wind picked up, moaning as a storm approached. The waves grew larger, breaking against the hull, and the *Berenice* rocked and swayed roughly. A strange, ominous hue, a weird color I'd never seen before, filled the darkening sky.

"Lower the mainsail," Dad ordered, as a sudden, much stronger, burst of wind tore a slice in a sail.

Jolene, Pierre-Paul, and I were no longer allowed on the deck. Not that we wanted to be out where some gusts were strong enough to launch us out to sea.

Hours passed. The waves grew larger still. The wind roared and sprayed water everywhere. The *Berenice* lurched, jerking this way and that.

The waves behaved strangely. Instead of moving in one direction in nice orderly rows, the waves came from all directions. They collided into each other. Sometimes two waves knocked each other into nothingness. Other times, they merged into a super wave, bigger than all the rest.

An unbelievably strong wind pushed the men working on the deck. They fought to stand upright, but gusts slammed them, sometimes knocking them over. The waves came faster and faster. Now the waves were taller than any man, yet they continued to swell, growing larger and larger.

The storm pushed our vessel along too quickly. If we didn't slow down, the force of the mighty storm would shred our sails, break the mast, capsize and sink our yacht. Dad ordered first one sail down, and then another and another, until only one sail, the genoa jib, remained. One little sail gave the men some control over our direction, but even with just one sail up, we flew along going more than sixty knots—more than seventy miles per hour by land measurements.

Waves towered over the deck. The bilge had to be pumped nonstop, so the *Berenice* didn't fill with water and sink. The waves and wind continued to grow. The storm we encountered before Christmas Island was a cuddly kitten compared to this roaring lion.

Falling asleep that night, I hoped to awaken to calm the next morning. We all thought the storm would be over soon, but the next morning, the blow had intensified. Waves now towered over Dad's head and reached halfway up the mast. The wind was strong enough that we feared that a sudden gust might snap the masts in two.

My stomach sloshed about. I longed for fresh air, but I didn't dare leave the cabin.

"Forget staying on course. Dodge those waves. If one of those monsters collapses on us, we'll sink. Dart between them," Dad ordered as Claude took over the helm for a few minutes. "Just go whichever direction it takes to keep those mountains from falling on us," he repeated.

Dad dashed into the cabin for a quick bathroom break. When he exited the head, Mom shoved some hot food at him. Dad waved the food away, but Mom insisted.

"Don't have time," Dad yelled over the bellowing noises of the storm.

"Claude can manage for a minute," Mom replied.

Dad shoveled a couple of bites quickly into his mouth. His eyes lost their focus and his head nodded for a moment. Then he jerked awake again.

"Why don't you take a catnap?" Mom suggested.

"Can't. Storm's too fierce. Have to get back up there." He devoured another bite.

"Did you get any sleep last night?" she asked, worriedly, as she refilled his cup.

With a slight shake of his head, he hurried back on deck. He wasn't about to leave his post for long, despite having been on duty for most of two days and a night.

Time dragged for us children down below. Darkness, like a heavy damp blanket, weighed us down, smothered us, and made it impossible to see much. Roaring waves and howling winds made conversation difficult. The lurching, rolling, pitching of the ship made merely sitting on a berth a major chore. The damp, stale air smelled like a wet dog and a touch of mildew.

I found a corner, a tiny space, to wedge myself into. Jolene squeezed in beside me. We sat, finding comfort in squeezing close. Playing with toys was impossible. Reading or telling stories wouldn't work either. Instead, we just held on. It was hard to tell when night fell given the darkness of the days, but eventually we fell asleep while the adults battled on.

I awoke to darkness. The wind thundered louder than ever. Jerking and lurching pummeled the ship still. It seemed as though we'd lived this way forever.

Suddenly the *Berenice* tipped over. Way, way over. She was about to flip upside down!

"We're heeling. Lower the genoa jib!" yelled Dad, dashing from the head. Flying out into the nightmare, he yelled, "Raise the staysail!"

Somehow, the boat righted herself. We were still upright. We hadn't capsized. Not this time, anyway.

For three days and two nights, the storm raged with only brief lulls. I couldn't see much through the portholes even when there was enough light. The waves were so tall; they had to bend down, far down, to touch the top of the mast. They seemed to reach the sky.

I tried to keep Jolene and Pierre-Paul busy to give me something else to think about, but it didn't work anymore. The storm was too dark, too noisy, and battered us too violently.

Hours slowly passed. A violent punch of wind knocked the *Berenice* onto its side again. Dad ordered the last sail down just as it ripped into shreds.

"The dinghy!" Claude pointed at the small rowboat that hung from a wooden frame over the stern. Full of water, the weight of the little boat pulled the *Berenice*'s stern down into the sea, and threatened to pull the yacht under, stern first, and sink us all.

"A knife! Give me a knife!" Dad screamed as he scrambled back to the stern. There was no time to unwrap the ropes from the cleats. The lines would have to be cut.

Someone slapped a knife in his hand. Dad struggled, pushing against the wind, trying to reach the stern. Somehow, with much effort, he reached it. Grabbing the wooden frame that angled out over the sea, knife clenched between his teeth, he crawled far enough up the support to reach the rope. He sawed desperately with the knife. The rope snapped in two. The dinghy teetered for a moment and then plunged into the sea, disappearing from sight in a flash as the *Berenice* bounced from the force of the dinghy's plummet.

Dad and the crew scurried about in their yellow foul-weather gear. They'd worn the heavy vinyl raincoats and rain pants for days. With both hands on the wheel, straining with his shoulders and thigh muscles, Dad wrenched the *Berenice* first this way and then that, dodging one mountainous wave after another. At times, another man held the wheel with him. Together they pooled their strength to steer against the storm.

The *Berenice*, without any sails up, still raced along too quickly. From a storage area in the bow where anchors, sails and other equipment were kept, Bill and Claude hoisted a couple of old car tires. Tying a rope to each, they flung them over the stern. The dragging tires would act as brakes, slowing us down. We hoped these sea anchors would slow us enough that we could maintain control and outlast this tempest.

Mom stayed below. She cared for Jackie and kept busy cooking meals for everyone. She made meals on the wildly swinging kerosene stove to keep up everyone's strength and spirits, though I for one didn't feel much like eating. I was seasick from the horrendous storm that had rocked us so viciously for days. The grownups barely touched their food, either. They had too much work to do, too many worries to take time out for food.

Another night passed. Would this storm ever end? Four days and three nights, it had raged. None of the adults had slept except for a brief nap or two. Too busy trying to keep us afloat, they barely had time to sit for a minute.

Eventually, it was too much. Exhaustion took its toll. Their eyes were dark hollows. The grownups were sluggish, making mistakes, too tired to think straight anymore, too tired to even stand anymore. They couldn't go on. Physically couldn't do it.

"We need sleep. Can't do this any longer. Let's say a prayer and get some rest," Dad said with an air of defeat.

No one argued with him.

We had barely managed to stay afloat when the adults did everything they could to dodge the waves. Without their constant efforts, how on earth would the *Berenice* not end up buried underneath one of those humongous waves? How could we survive the night with no one on watch? But they were too exhausted. Dad said a final prayer for all of us, asking for mercy on our souls. He didn't expect to wake up the next morning. He didn't think we'd outlive this never-ending storm.

13. Where Are We?

To everyone's surprise, morning had come. The world was calmer. The wind was still incredibly strong, but it no longer knocked the *Berenice* about like a punching bag between two boxing champions. The waves were huge, but they no longer reached the sky. The storm that had lasted for days, that seemed endless, was finally weakening.

Our dinghy was gone. Mom tossed Jackie's sleeping basket overboard as the storm had battered it beyond recognition. Most of the sails were shredded. The cement hull, strong as it was, had been pummeled so badly that a section of cement had been blasted into chunks. Thankfully, the chicken wire frame inside the concrete held the chunks in place, so the leak was manageable. More importantly, we were alive. We'd made it through the night. As long as the bilge was pumped constantly, we wouldn't sink.

"But where are we?" Dad muttered as he sat in the closet-like navigation room. He stared at his charts. We'd zigzagged so much—dodging monstrous waves, trying to survive—that it was impossible to say which direction we'd eventually gone. We may have gone in circles for all we knew. How far had the storm pushed us? Since the storm began more than a week ago, dark clouds, towering waves, and the constant lurching of the deck made it impossible for Dad to take a sight with his sextant, impossible to calculate where we were. Even now, with the storm dying, dark clouds hid the sun. Dad still couldn't use his sextant to calculate where we were.

After a few minutes, Dad muttered to himself, "We'll head northwest. Bound to hit Asia or Africa. Eventually."

Of course Africa and Asia were large enough that we'd eventually find one of them, but that could take weeks. We desperately needed to make repairs. We couldn't limp that far in this condition. Until the weather cleared enough for him to use his sextant and figure out exactly where we were, it was impossible to plot a course to a smaller destination. Asia or Africa was the best we could do for now.

14. A Fish Story

The storm wasn't completely gone. The wind was stiff, and the *Berenice* trucked along at a fast clip, but the rain had stopped. The waves settled into a more orderly pattern so our motion was much smoother. The weather was calm enough that Dad let the crew take turns at the helm once more. Despite a couple of nights of sleep, the adults were still tired. Physically, they looked as beaten down as though they'd just come out of a heavyweight boxing championship, but they were elated to be alive.

Bill had a gift for talking people into things. On Christmas Island, he'd begged some toilet paper and fishing gear off sailors on another vessel.

"Why not try a relaxing bout of fishing?" Bill suggested from his seat at the tiller. "You need the rest, and we need the food." Thus, Dad tried his hand at fishing for one of the first times in our four-month voyage.

Dad tied a hook to the end of the fishing line. Then he put on the thick, leather hand-protector that he used when making sail repairs. We had no fishing rod, just plain old fishing line. That's why he needed the hand-protector: To keep the fishing line from slicing his hand as it slid across his palm.

Throwing the hook over the stern, he let it trail behind as we cruised speedily along. Dad settled back to wait, holding the line in his protected hand, as he closed his eyes and rested his weary body, leaning against the side of the aft cabin.

It didn't take long. The line jerked. Dad sat bolt upright as the line slid across the leather, more and more of it speeding into the ocean. When the line stopped racing, Dad grabbed it with both hands, and started to pull it in. He tugged first with one hand. Then he grabbed and heaved some more with the other hand. One hand, then the other pulled, stopping only to wind the line around a reel. Whatever was on the other end of the line didn't put up with that for long. It didn't want to be dragged anywhere. The line jerked again. Dad caught himself in time so he wasn't pulled over the side.

"Need help?" Claude wandered back to watch the action.

"Be nice," Dad grunted, pressing his feet against the deck for traction as he struggled to hold the line racing away from him.

I changed position in the companionway to get a better view. If I stayed out of their way, I hoped I wouldn't be sent below and miss out on the action. Squinting, I looked far out to sea behind us. The sun glinted off something moving. Staring intently, I saw a tiny fish leap out of the ocean, flipping this way and that, before it disappeared into the water.

Marie took over the tiller, so Bill could help, too. Two of the grown men heaved on the fishing line, while the third kept the line from tangling. Even with three of them working in tandem, they strained to draw in the creature. The fish reappeared closer to the *Berenice*, and then closer. Then it yanked the line hard, and all three men scrambled to keep their footing. The line zipped through their hands as the animal sped away. The fish seemed to be winning this tug-of-war contest.

They let it race until the end of the tough transparent fishing line drew near. Taking a few deep breaths, they shook their arms, stretched their backs, and began again. Heaving on the line, they reeled in more and more, once again pulling the fish closer and closer. Just when it was nearer than ever, the fish regained its strength, and tugged the line once more.

Jumping high out of the water, flipping this way and that, jerking, fighting to be free of the hook pulling at its mouth, the magnificent creature was quite a sight to behold. Again and again, it leapt high above the water, the sun glinting off its silvery back. Finally, the fish fell into the water and stayed there for a while. The men took advantage as the fish grew tired and pulled on the line again, steadily tugging it closer, and closer.

I gasped as I jumped to my feet on the step where I was perched. Without thinking, I yelled, "Oh, my!" So much for keeping quiet and going unnoticed, but the men concentrated so hard on their task that they paid no attention. When the fish unexpectedly rose out of the water, much closer than before, it had finally hit me that this fish wasn't tiny at all. The animal still wasn't near enough for me to hit it with a ball, if I'd had one to throw, but even from this distance, that thing was huge. A giant. I'd never seen a fish so big.

The fish hadn't given up. It jolted, jumped, flipped, and dove deeper. The fishing line sped through the men's hands as the bolting fish plunged deeper and deeper into the Indian Ocean.

Eventually, I grew tired of watching the same thing repeatedly. I'm not sure how long the fishing adventure had lasted so far, but nothing new seemed likely to happen any time soon. Besides, the wind picked up, and rain fell once more. The storm hadn't completely disappeared, yet, so I took refuge below deck, intending to ask for a snack. Mom had damper spread with Vegemite ready. Yum!

Vegemite sandwiches were as popular with Australian kids as peanut butter ones were with American children. Brownish-black, smooth like soft-spread margarine, made with vegetable extract and Brewer's yeast, Vegemite was a sandwich spread full of B-vitamins. Most Americans took one smell and refused to try it, but I loved the tangy taste that reminded me of soy sauce.

After the snack, Jolene and I played with dolls for a while. Then I read some animal stories from one of my thick green-covered Disney books. Later, Jolene, Pierre-Paul, and I built with blocks—though I kept a careful eye on Pierre-Paul to make sure he didn't run off with any more of them. He soon grew bored and went off to play by himself. Eventually, the weather cleared again, and I returned to my post at the top of the steps to watch the fishing.

The men had been fishing for hours now. Blood smeared the palms of their hands where the fishing line had sliced them. Their sun-bronzed bodies were drenched with pungent sweat. Occasional grunts, groans, and Dad's cries of "heave" to help them pull in unison, punctuated their silence.

Though the fish was closer than when I'd left, it was still more than two boat-lengths away. The fight had taken a toll on it, too. The fish still leapt, flipped, and twisted this way and that, but not as vigorously. It rested longer and more often. Tiring, it slowly drew closer and closer. It was twenty yards away. Then fifteen. Then ten yards. Now it was only twenty feet away.

A sudden burst of energy exploded from the fish, and it took off, racing away. The spurt of energy didn't last long. Soon, Dad yelled "heave" and the men again pulled the line. The animal was only thirty feet away. Then twenty. Now ten feet from the hull. Finally, Bill reached down with a gaff and used the curved hook on the end of the pole to help lift the creature up onto the hull. Dad and Claude pulled on the line until they could bend down and grab the beast. Grunting and groaning, the three of them dumped the fish onto the deck.

Water splashed as the fish hit the deck, but the deck wasn't slippery. Not really. Months ago, back in Hervey Bay, before our voyage had begun, Dad sprinkled sand onto the wet paint on the deck. The sand gave traction even when wet feet hit the smooth, damp concrete, so the fish didn't slide much.

The men, breathing hard, hunched over the monstrous beast. It jerked and flipped wildly again. Claude clunked it on the head. The fish slumped, and the men collapsed onto the deck. Eyes closed and panting, the three fellows remained there for several minutes. Finally, they peeled themselves off the deck.

"That's a fair dinkum catch!" Bill caressed his raw, bloody hands. Then he grinned. "Worth going fishing for that one!"

Claude asked, "What is it?"

"Looks like a yellow-fin tuna." Dad held his hands out. Mom gently took the leather hand-protector off one hand and cleaned the torn flesh on the other.

Cocking his head, Dad studied the captive for a minute. "It must weigh a hundred and fifty pounds."

"No wonder it was so hard to reel in," Claude muttered.

Bill added, "No one will believe we reeled it in on a hand line."

Heads down, they stared silently at it for a minute, considering those words.

Marie broke the silence. "Wait a minute!" She turned and disappeared through the cabin door. A minute later, she reappeared with a Polaroid Instamatic Camera.

Soon, Jolene, Pierre-Paul, and I sat in front of the tuna that was much larger than the three of us put together. Marie snapped photos and handed them out. Bill got a copy, as did each family.

Looking at the colorful photo that appeared on the paper ejected by the camera, Bill said, "Proof that it's no fish story."

How could we store so much tuna? Some went into the teeny, tiny refrigerator that Mom powered up especially for the fish. The men sliced quite a bit into thin strips that they salted and hung out to dry in the sun. The fish jerky wouldn't need refrigeration.

Despite the huge amounts they sliced off, most of the animal remained. There was simply too much for the nine of us to eat. Well, eight of us since Jackie was too young to eat solid food yet. Most of the catch was tossed overboard, to the delight of a group of sharks that followed us for days afterwards, hoping for another feast.

I loved canned tuna, which was one of the few forms of canned protein we could readily buy in those days. A lot of it was stored inside the bases of the berths.

Yet fresh tuna tasted different. It was better somehow. Tuna steaks made a wonderful supper that night, a delicious change of pace from canned food. Breakfast the next morning was a good slab of pan-fried tuna. There was as much tuna as anyone wanted to eat. No restrictions. For lunch, we had tuna again. Tuna was on the menu three times a day, day after day. Tuna wasn't so tasty anymore.

"Are you alright?" Mom asked Marie on the fourth day of our all-tuna diet. Marie's face was blotchy and red. Her arms and legs were, too, and she scratched repeatedly.

"Let me get Wally to take a look at you," Mom said before rushing off to find Dad.

"Turn around," Dad ordered Marie. He looked her up and down, studying the pattern of red on her back. Looking at Mom with a grim expression, he asked, "Anyone else have it?"

While Marie had the most obvious case, the rest of us were developing a rash, too.

"Must be the tuna. That's all we've been eating. Best dump what's left before it gets worse."

My parents rarely wasted food. Especially out here where there were no grocery stores, no farms. In fact, when Mom accidentally dropped food, she brushed it off and served it anyway, but Dad didn't want to poison anyone.

We didn't fish for a while after that. Fishing was too painful, too much work, and too wasteful since we could eat only a tiny fraction of the huge fish that roamed these deep waters. Besides, we didn't want dozens of hungry sharks following us.

Like many sailors, Dad worried about sharks. We never wore the life jackets that boats were required to carry. Dad said that if one of us ever fell overboard, he'd rescue us pronto—if possible. If he couldn't, drowning quickly was preferable to being ripped apart and eaten alive by sharks.

For now, we had other problems to deal with. We hadn't recovered from the massive storm, which hadn't completely disappeared. It reappeared every few hours, a little weaker each time. The hull leaked. Most of our sails were shredded. Our spinnaker pole was lost, and we still didn't know where we were.

Those weren't the only concerns. Our food supplies were lower than expected. The huge stash of food, which had filled every storage area when we left Darwin, was disappearing faster than expected. The crew ate much more than twice what we'd expected, although no one grew fat. Hard work and fresh sea air worked up hearty appetites. The crew helped occasionally with supplies though my parents worried that they weren't overly scrupulous about where they obtained them. It didn't help that engine repairs had required chunks of money that should have been reserved for supplies. Mom used the last of the eggs from Christmas Island; none had spoiled without refrigeration. The honey and syrup were gone, and our flour was running low. We still had powdered milk, sacks of rice and potatoes, jars of Vegemite, and plenty of cans of beans, steak-and-kidney pie, and formula. We had dozens of cans of tuna, too, though no one wanted to touch those. We'd be fine for weeks still, and if worst came to worst, we could go fishing again, though we weren't ready to try that again just yet.

Freshwater was another concern. The freshwater tanks were slowly emptying. We could replenish our water supply a little at sea with buckets of rainwater—if rain fell without accompanying storm winds—though that rarely happened. We couldn't live long without freshwater, but we should have enough to last us to the next port. We hoped.

15. On to Diego Garcia

The next day, the weather settled enough for Dad to take a sight. Finally, he calculated where we were. We'd blown past the Cocos Islands—our intended port of call. According to our charts, the nearest refuge was a small French island, Diego Garcia, about a thousand miles south of India in a group of islands called the Chagos Archipelago.

On October 5, almost three weeks after the huge storm first struck, Diego Garcia drew near, but something wasn't right.

"Hey, look, a ship!" Bill yelled excitedly, pointing behind our stern.

Dad pulled out his binoculars. "Looks like a fishing trawler. Nice to have company. Wonder if they'll come any closer?"

Half an hour later, the boat was no nearer.

Repeatedly, Dad checked on the fishing boat. "Very odd," he said a couple of hours later, as he dropped the binoculars to let them hang around his neck.

"What's odd?" Claude asked from where he took his turn at the bilge pump.

"That fishing boat. If I didn't know better, I'd swear it was following us. It never gets any closer. It seems to follow our every movement, but always stays the same distance away."

"Land ho! Looks like Diego Garcia," Dad yelled some time later from his perch on the mast.

"Finally!"

"Hooray!"

We were excited to reach a safe haven where we could make much-needed repairs, rest, and take on freshwater and other supplies, as well as stretch our legs and get away from each other for a bit of much needed privacy.

As we drew nearer, Marie became thoughtful and quiet. Her brows knit, she looked warily at the island and then back at the fishing boat that followed farther away now. "I don't know," she said slowly. "Are you sure this is a plantation? It doesn't look like a native village."

"There's a lot of activity for a small island community, but the charts say it's a French plantation," Dad said, as he studied the situation. Gray steel ships filled the harbor. Machinery moved about on the island. Uniformed men roamed the beach.

"May I see the binoculars?" Marie asked. "My father is a diplomat. I have lived in many countries. From what I see," she said, handing the binoculars back to Dad, "I believe this is a military base."

"In the never-never?" Bill scoffed. "Who'd put a military base out in the middle of the ocean?"

What was going on? Would it be safe to land here? We had no choice. The adults were still exhausted, and we desperately needed to make repairs.

"Leave the area immediately!" boomed a voice through a megaphone. A swift, gray military ship stopped a few yards away. Weapons were visible on deck. Stern faces stared down at us, but the stars and stripes told us they were American.

Standing on deck, legs spread apart, Dad used his hands as a make-shift megaphone. "We need to make repairs!"

"This is an American naval base. A war zone. No civilians allowed. Leave the area immediately," the uniformed man repeated.

Our charts were outdated. The British had taken over the French plantation, just the previous year, and leased it to the American military. This out-of-the-way island was closer to Vietnam, where a war was underway, than any other American base. (Later, it would be the closest American base to a war in Iraq.) The Americans were busy building a military base, planning battles, transporting men and machines to and from that deadly war.

"We're American citizens. We have a right to land," Dad persisted.

I knew that look on his face—the one that said stand back because he was coming through and don't mess with him—but apparently the sailor didn't recognize the expression.

"No civilians allowed. No women or children on the island. We're fighting a war," the man insisted.

More uniformed men gathered near the fellow with the megaphone. They were all armed, but at least the guns weren't aimed at us. Not yet, anyway.

"I'm an honorably discharged veteran. U.S. Air Force," Dad snapped. "We need to make repairs. Storm damage. I demand to speak to your superior."

The man lowered his megaphone and turned to another man. After a brief conversation, he nodded to a third who darted off and disappeared. After a few tense moments, another man—a man clearly in charge—strode onto the deck. The small crowd parted to let him through. He extended his hand and the megaphone was promptly handed to him.

"I'm in charge here," he said, introducing himself. "Did you say you were damaged in the storm?"

"Yes, sir."

"In the huge storm that passed by recently?" he repeated, his voice rising an octave. Behind the megaphone, his jaw dropped and eyebrows rose.

"Yes, sir," Dad repeated, impatiently. "We need to make repairs."

"B-b-but . . . You were out in that? You made it through a cyclone in that little sailboat?"

A cyclone is the southern hemisphere's version of a hurricane. Our homemade thirty-nine foot ferro-cement yacht had survived the sort of storm that can destroy entire cities. We'd survived and lived to tell the tale. The *Berenice* had proven herself one very tough vessel. Now, we just wanted to make the repairs needed to continue our journey.

16. A Military Base

The base commander himself eventually gave us permission to land at Diego Garcia long enough to make the most necessary repairs. Once the *Berenice* was raised out of the water, Dad fixed the leaky hull using the bag of quick-drying cement that he kept onboard for emergencies. Stirring some water into the gray mix of rocks, sand, and other dirty looking stuff, he made a paste resembling thick lumpy pancake batter, which he smeared on and around the chunks of broken concrete, completely sealing the area. It took several days to complete the repairs and test the hull to be sure no leaks remained.

In the meantime, uniformed Americans escorted the women and us children around the base. We weren't allowed anywhere without armed guards.

"Could we take a shower, please?" Mom asked the base commander, who greeted us outside his headquarters.

"Sorry, Ma'am. That would be a problem. There are no women on the base. No facilities for women," the commander replied. Standing ramrod straight with legs spread slightly, he was courteous but firm as he denied the request. "No telling what the men would do if women used their showers. Some haven't seen women or children in a long time. Just back from the war in Vietnam and many will return soon. Just can't chance it." He shook his head.

"Please, we are dying for a shower. We have not had a decent bath in weeks," begged Marie. Holding his arm, she looked up at him with large, tear-filled eyes. "A freshwater shower . . . It has been so long. It would feel so wonderful. Please?"

"Please?" Mom repeated. "We can't shower on the deck with all the men about." Out at sea, we bathed on deck; otherwise, the head stunk of mold and mildew. The women and girls went first, while the men and Pierre-Paul stayed below. We took sponge baths from buckets of seawater, unless a light rainfall pattered on us. Saltwater baths removed dirt and grime but left a gritty, sticky residue on the skin. The women longed for the fresh, clean feeling of a freshwater shower, though we'd never waste precious drinking water on baths.

"All right, ladies." The commander said slowly. "I'll see what I can manage, but I'm not making any promises."

Later that day, the commander ordered all the men out of a building. After he verified it was empty, he posted armed guards with guns held at the ready, around the perimeter of the building, to keep any men from sneaking in. Then, the commander himself led us inside and stood outside the bathroom door, holding a loaded machine gun. With all this security in place, we finally enjoyed a luxurious freshwater shower.

Afterward, other uniformed men escorted us children around the base while the grownups attended to business. Our guards, dressed in uniforms of several shades of green and brown, were friendly despite the weapons at their sides, and they entertained us as best they could.

"Want to ride in a jeep?" One of them pointed to an open-topped green vehicle.

After being cooped up for most of three weeks, we were full of energy and ready for excitement. We nodded enthusiastically and, with a bit of help, scrambled into the back, while the men climbed into the front seats.

The slender young men drove across the base, onto the beach and all around. We waved whenever we passed other military men, and they all stopped what they were doing, looking surprised to see children cheerfully greet them as though peace reigned. The scent of dust and fuel, the feel of the breeze and occasional bits of sand blowing in our faces, and the sun warming our faces felt so wonderful after three weeks of damp darkness onboard.

"How about we do something else?" the man behind the steering wheel asked, before shifting gears and taking off in another direction. He said something to the man sitting beside him, but I couldn't understand it over the noise of the motor.

Next thing I knew, the jeep stopped on the beach of a sheltered cove. The men helped us down to the sand and led us to a tiny boat at the water's edge. This boat was nothing like the military boats that dotted the harbor. It wasn't painted gray but was instead a cheerful light blue. Tiny, it could only hold four or maybe five adults. Jolene, Pierre-Paul, and I sat in the back of the low-riding cabin-less boat. It resembled a dinghy but had no outboard motor, no oars, nor any sails. Instead, there were two sets of bicycle-style pedals on the floor under the dashboard. This boat moved with pedal power!

With a push from another fellow on the beach, our boat glided into a tranquil cove as our escorts pedaled smoothly. We heard the sounds of the whirring pedals, our own voices, the soft shushing as water streamed past our hull, and little else. The huge naval ships and the hustle and bustle of the base seemed far, far away.

"Would one of you like to pedal?" one of the guys asked.

"Yes, please," we yelled.

One of sailors climbed over his seat, balancing himself and stepping gently as he tried to rock the boat as little as possible. Standing with one foot on each side of the small craft, he lifted me over to the empty front seat. Perched on the chair's edge, I stretched to reach the pedals. At first, I couldn't move them. They required much more force than did my bike back in Australia. Pushing again, with all my might, the boat moved a tiny bit. When my co-pilot, the other sailor, pedaled too, the job became much easier.

My co-pilot demonstrated how to use the metal handle to steer. It looked easy when he did it, but when I used the tiller, the boat went in circles. When I turned the handle the other direction, to stop the circles, the boat circled the opposite direction instead.

Our escorts laughed good-naturedly at my attempts and offered some suggestions. With a smile beaming across his face, one said we reminded him of his little girl back in the States. The other talked about his little sister.

When Jolene and Pierre-Paul were given turns, the pedals under the dashboard were too far for their shorter legs to reach. Jolene hopped off the seat and tried crouching under the dashboard to pedal, but that didn't work either. Finally, the men said not to worry about pedaling, and so the little ones figured out how to steer while one of our guards pedaled for them. Later, Jolene and I squeezed onto a seat together, and I pedaled while she steered.

"Oh, thank you so much," I cried when we returned to the beach.

"That was lots of fun," Jolene added.

Pierre-Paul didn't say anything. I wasn't surprised, since good manners weren't his style.

Arriving back at the *Berenice*, we were exhausted from the fun and excitement of the day, as well as the fatigue remaining from our long battle against the cyclone. We went to bed early and slept late the next morning, secure in a safe harbor.

At breakfast, Mom told Dad about our armed escorts. "They're very nice men. Very pleasant."

"Glad to hear it." Dad took another bite of the rice we ate with reconstituted powdered milk and sugar as a homemade breakfast cereal.

"Well, some of them asked if they could help us out, give us some supplies or something. They knew we had a rough time of it, knew we'd been hoping to stock up at a market here."

"At least the base let us fill the water tanks," Dad said, nodding. "What'd you say to them? They could get in trouble giving away government property."

"I know, dear, but they kept insisting. I finally told them we'd love a loaf of bread, fair dinkum yeast bread."

"That should be all right, I suppose," Dad said slowly, nodding thoughtfully.

"Oh, and that fishing boat that followed us?" Mom added. "It's a Russian spy ship. Apparently, it keeps an eye on everyone who comes here."

Soon after, the guards assigned to watch us this morning came on duty.

One held his hat in his hands, spinning it nervously. "You said you could use some bread, ma'am. We got together, several of us, and brought you some."

"Do you mind if I set this on your deck?" Another carried a medium-sized cardboard box to our ketch. Rather than the single loaf of bread Mom had hoped for, they presented us with a box full of fresh bread and some lunchmeat.

Over the next four days, Dad and the men finished the most pressing repairs. Dad mended a few sails, sewing ripped sections together again with heavy thread. The hole in the cement hull was sealed. With the most necessary repairs made, officials on Diego Garcia insisted we move on. They worried about the security of their military base and didn't want civilians around any longer than necessary.

As we prepared to put out to sea again, a group of men approached. "We brought something for you. We thought maybe . . . Well, we hope the kids like these," a brown-haired young man said, holding out another brown cardboard box.

"They're for all of you, ma'am," a soldier with a crew cut added, nodding at Mom and Marie.

"You shouldn't have done that," Dad said. He was reluctant to take the gift. He knew that soldiers in a war zone don't have much for themselves, let alone extras to give away, and he didn't want to steal military supplies, either.

"We all pitched in, sir. They're from our rations. Hope you'll enjoy them," one explained.

"You remind us of our loved ones back home, sir. It's like giving us a chance to help our own," a third soldier added, as he nodded his head and shuffled his feet uncomfortably.

With that, Dad accepted their precious gift, and what a gift it was. The large box was full of little packages of M&Ms. I'd never seen so much candy before. We hadn't had chocolate in months. We were so excited, looking forward to enjoying the treats. Little did we know the trouble those M&Ms would cause.

17. The Deserted Island

Oct. 12, 1971

"Hmm, makes no sense to backtrack to the Cocos Islands. Cyclone blew us past those," Dad muttered as he sat in his tiny navigation room studying the charts.

Mom stood a few feet away in the galley, preparing dinner. "Oh!" she yelped. "Sorry, dear, a little crab came through the saltwater faucet; it startled me." Mom dumped that batch of seawater in the sink. Then she pumped more water into the pot and added some chopped potatoes. "So where to, then?"

"Well, it doesn't make sense to head to Indochina, as planned," Dad continued. "We've gone so far west already, we might as well head over to Africa. Besides, Vietnam's in Indochina. I don't want to head into a war."

"No stops until Africa?" Mom asked. Despite the rest on Diego Garcia, her shoulders slumped and she moved slowly. Like the other adults, she was still exhausted.

"We'll find a couple of islands along the way. Stop in the Seychelles somewhere, but our next major destination will be Durban, South Africa." Dad nodded, and used his calipers to measure off the distance. "How about a stop tonight at Egmont Island? Seems a nice place for some rest. We won't go far in this weather, anyway."

Thankfully, the outer bands of the cyclone had swept past the area leaving behind beautifully calm weather. Too calm. The wind was so light, we barely moved. Relaxing and recuperating on a beautiful, tropical island seemed a perfect way to wait for a better wind.

In the late afternoon, Bill called from his perch atop the mast, "Land!"

A day after leaving Diego Garcia, we sunk anchor at Egmont Island. Still in the Chagos Island group, Egmont was deserted. No people lived here—at least, not anymore. We sailed into a tranquil lagoon where shallow water lapped sandy shores. Lush jungle, a wall of greenery with lots of palm trees, coconut palms, banana plants, vines, and plants I didn't recognize filled the area beyond the beach. Birds called in the distance. Bright, tropical fish darted in the crystal clear water surrounding us. This was the stuff of dreams.

The cyclone had devoured our dinghy, so Dad improvised. He tied a rope to the *Berenice*. Wrapping its other end over one shoulder, he jumped over the side and swam ashore. He tied the rope's loose end to a palm tree that bent over the lagoon. Swimming back to the *Berenice*, he climbed aboard and told the crew to blow up a large black tube, while he looped a thinner rope over the first rope and made a loose noose around it. When the tube was ready, he tied the other end of the thin rope around it and tossed the tube into the calm water.

"We've got a ferry now." He pointed at his device. "Who wants to go first?"

"I'll go," said Claude.

"Me, too. I see coconuts and papayas. Fresh fruit for supper!" Bill rubbed his hands together.

One by one, the men climbed down onto the black tube. All three sat, bare feet dangling in the water. Dad reached up and grabbed the overhead rope. Pulling, hand over hand, he drew the ferry to shore.

The men soon scrambled onto shore. Bill and Claude shimmied up trees and tossed fresh fruit down to Dad. They returned laden with bananas, coconuts, papayas, and other delicious fruit. Since leaving Christmas Island, the only fruit we'd had was canned. We'd had little fresh fruit since leaving mainland Australia, so this was a wonderful treat. After numerous attempts with a large knife, the men figured out how to open the coconuts, and we soon drank coconut milk and ate coconut meat. We devoured bananas and papayas, eating our fill of fruit. No rations. No worries about eating too much and depleting our supplies.

After supper, as the sun sank over the horizon, we dropped into bed. We lived by the light of the sun, not wanting to waste the kerosene that powered our lamps and the stove. The adults were still exhausted from the many sleepless stormy nights, and the time spent at Diego Garcia, making hurried repairs, hadn't helped them much.

The next morning, we went ashore for a much-needed vacation. Bill, Claude, and Dad waded in the shallow water of the cove. Small sand sharks, two or three feet long, startled them, nipping harmlessly at their ankles until they shook them off. Shuffling their feet across the sandy bottom, clouds of sand flew up, sending warning to stingrays, crabs, and other creatures that darted out of their way. They planned to catch something fresh for dinner. Something caught here, in the shallow water, wouldn't be as overwhelmingly large as the tuna.

Bill produced a harpoon that he'd talked someone into giving him. Together the three men scouted around, looking for a nice-sized fish to spear. After a while, they stood still, letting the sand settle and the water grow still around them. They hunched over, scanning the water for a suitable target. Silently, one pointed when he spotted a possibility. Watching, they waited for the right moment to strike, but every time they shot, the fish dashed out of the way and disappeared before the swirling water cleared. They retrieved the spear and tried, again and again, without success. None of them had used a harpoon before, and it showed.

Suddenly, Bill bent down and slammed the palm of his hand into the water, splashing Claude. Turning slightly, he splashed Dad, too. Stunned, the two men stood up straight. Then they laughed. It was a long time since I'd heard laughter. Dad loved to joke, teasing playfully, but the cyclone had changed that. Laughing and yelping, the three engaged in a light-hearted water battle, splashing each other like little boys.

Eventually the laughter died down, and they returned to the serious business of harpooning a fish for supper. Everything was too quick for them.

"Hey, what about those?" Claude whispered, pointing excitedly. Some spotted green turtles slowly glided across the water. "They're more our speed."

"Right!" Bill said quietly. "Isn't turtle soup a delicacy served in posh restaurants?" Slowly and quietly, he sloshed toward the turtles, harpoon held high, ready to fire. The harpoon novices speared one turtle and later a second. Triumphantly, the men pushed them toward the shore.

On the beach, Jolene and I searched for dried, broken branches or driftwood, while Pierre-Paul roamed idly about. Mom buried potatoes in the sand, and then stacked the wood we'd gathered over the potatoes, building a bonfire. With assistance from Marie, Mom cut out the turtle meat and cleaned their shells, turning one of the shells into a giant cooking pot in which she made turtle soup. Fresh fruit was prepared, too. We'd had shorter rations lately as Mom attempted to stretch our food supplies, so this abundant meal was a feast. When the soup was ready, Mom poked a stick into the sand and dug the potatoes out from where they'd baked under the bonfire. We sat on the sand and ate our meal by firelight—though I refused to touch the soup since I couldn't face the idea of eating turtle—as the sun set over the horizon.

The next morning, our mini-vacation continued. Just after sunrise, the women took us children on a hike along the beach. Kicking our feet in the water's edge, we examined creatures as we strolled along and poked at the sand with sticks.

After a while, Marie said, "I am ready to turn around. I want to lie on the beach and work on nothing but my tan and a nap. This walk is too much work."

"Oh, the island isn't big. I think I'd like to stroll around it," Mom said.

"Can we go back, too?" I asked. Soon the rest of us returned, giving Mom a vacation from child-care. She planned to be back before nightfall.

Marie lay on the beach in the sun. Pierre-Paul played nearby in the sand, and four-month-old Jackie slept peacefully on a blanket.

The men spent the morning on further repairs, but then they pulled their shirts off and dove into the water. They planned to spend the rest of the day swimming and relaxing.

"Can I explore the island?" I asked hopefully, pointing at the lush jungle beyond the sand. I'd wanted to explore an island for so long. Maybe I'd finally get to do it.

"All right. Just be careful. Don't get lost. And keep an eye on Jolene," Dad said.

"Come on," I said, pulling Jolene behind me. As usual, she was ready and willing to follow her big sister.

Finally, I was going to explore. Climbing over roots and low plants, I circled around some trees and ducked under low branches. We followed an overgrown path between the trees that led into the jungle. Perhaps people had lived here before and cleared this path, which had become overgrown after they quit using it. How exciting! I was a real explorer!

I pushed aside some large leaves to make my way through the forest. Vines, hanging from the trees, brushed my face. I scooted under them when I could, pushed past them if I couldn't. I worked my way slowly, careful not to step on anything nasty with my bare feet, scanning the area for snakes, prickly plants, or sharp rocks. The scent of fresh fruit mingled with the damp aroma of dirt and plants.

Reaching a clearing the size of a small room, I stopped and listened. Birds called to each other. Leaves rustled as unseen creatures scrambled away from us. The canopy of leaves overhead blocked much of the sunlight. The sounds from the beach were muffled. I felt as though I'd stepped into another world.

Jolene was behind me. Not as cautious, she didn't worry about hurting her bare feet or about lurking dangers. Yet she was slower, pulling leaves aside and looking under them as we went. She probably searched for worms or bugs of some kind. Maybe she wanted to find a pet. Occasionally I stopped to let her catch up, or at least urged her to hurry up.

I pushed onward, but then halted. Something caught my eye in one of the trees. A ray of sunlight glinted off something. That was odd. What could it be? Cautiously, I moved closer.

"Wow! Look at that!" I called to Jolene, urging her to come closer. I pointed to the curious sight.

Right in front of us, was a tree unlike any I'd ever seen before. The tree itself wasn't strange. Rather it was what hung from it. Bits of rope or twine dangled from several branches, and at the end of each was a glass bottle. Inside each bottle was a rolled-up piece of paper. I'd heard of people throwing bottles into the ocean with messages tucked inside them, but I'd never heard of a tree full of such bottles.

Jolene and I ran back to the beach. This was too big to keep to ourselves. Besides, we weren't sure what to make of it.

"Dad! Come! You'll never guess what we found! A bottle tree! A bottle tree!" I yelled.

Everyone on the beach looked up, wondering why the fuss. The men sloshed out of the water. Marie and Pierre-Paul dusted the sand off their swimming togs and wandered over. Dad asked a few questions, trying to figure out why I was so excited. Finally, the men followed us to the clearing.

After gaping at the tree for a while, Dad reached out and grabbed a bottle. Turning it upside-down, he carefully shook the paper out. He unrolled the piece of paper and read aloud a note from people who visited the island previously. He read their boat's name and origin, their names, where they headed, and the date they'd visited. Thrilled to hear about previous visitors to our deserted island, the note was passed around. We each examined it before Dad carefully rolled it and dropped it back in its bottle.

One by one, he pulled each note out of its bottle. Some slid out easily, while he used a stick and gently extracted others. Like the first, each bottle's note told of previous visitors who stopped at this lonely island as they cruised the Indian Ocean, far from civilization.

After reading them all, we tromped back to the beach, excitedly talking about our discovery. Dad ferried himself back to the yacht and grabbed an empty glass bottle, a length of twine, some paper, and a pencil. Together, we composed our own note, wanting to hang our own bit of history on the tree. Someday, future explorers would read about us. Maybe. Possibly.

Sunlight was fading, but Mom hadn't returned.

"Should we sail around the island to search for her?" Bill asked.

"No, it'll be too dark to see her from that far out. We might run into rocks or coral sailing so close to shore. Too dangerous," Dad said. After a few moments of silence, he announced, "I'll grab a lantern and go on foot. She headed east, so I'll go west. She was circling the island. I trust she's almost finished."

Heading toward the shoreline, he stopped. In the distance, a shadowy figure trudged toward us, along the water's edge.

"Mom!" Jolene and I yelled, running to greet her.

Mom sighed heavily and put out her arms for a hug. "Am I glad to see you!" She gave Dad a weary smile and jerked the ropes she held, so that two large green glass balls, somewhat larger than bowling balls, floated to the shoreline and lodged themselves in the sand.

"What're those?" I asked. "They look heavy."

"They're very heavy. I couldn't carry them or even drag them through the sand, so I've been towing them through the water." She looked down at them and then back at us. "I saw them floating offshore and waded out to see what they were. I still have no idea what they are, but they're so pretty. I thought we could keep them."

"You are not bringing those markers onboard. They weigh too much and take up too much space," Dad said, firmly.

"Markers? What do they mark?" Mom asked.

"Japanese fishermen mark their nets with them. They must have torn loose, probably during the cyclone that hit us, and drifted here. Forget about them." His face still looked grim. His eyes glared at her. "What took you so long, Carolyn? What happened out there?"

"At first I enjoyed the stroll around the island and the privacy, but then I realized I was trapped," Mom explained. "I didn't pay attention to the tide 'til the beach was covered in water. A rocky cliff lined that section of the shoreline and was too high for me to scale. I couldn't see how to get to the top. The water was too deep to wade through. Boulders were strewn about the base of the cliff. I climbed from one to another, but waves were crashing so; I was afraid they'd pound me into the rocks if the outgoing tide didn't sweep me out to sea. But I'd have swum if necessary," she added, bravely.

"Climbing across the rocks was slow work because they were so large and slippery. I was afraid I wouldn't make it back before dark and would have to spend the night alone on the rocks." She shuddered.

I imagined Mom huddled on a rock in the dark, sharks circling the water around her, wild beasts roaring from the jungle behind her, losing strength from hunger, soaking wet, and shivering in the dark. Thankfully, none of that happened and she found her way back to us before dark.

A ring-shaped coral reef had formed in the Indian Ocean, growing higher and higher until pieces of land emerged from the water and enclosed a peaceful lagoon. The pieces of land now known as Egmont Island, should have been named Egmont Atoll. Over time, some of the six original islands merged. Mapmakers—who hadn't visited the area for decades, if not hundreds of years—weren't sure how many separate pieces of land remained. Strolling around the island was difficult because it was not actually a single island.

Relieved to have Mom back, we returned to the *Berenice* in the dark. The men had stocked our yacht with as much fresh fruit as we could eat before it rotted. Tomorrow, after three restful days, we would leave our deserted island paradise and head toward Africa. However, this wouldn't be the last we'd hear of Egmont Island. Nor the last we'd hear of our bottle-tree discovery.

18. Through the Seychelles

Oct. 16, 1971

"The wind is getting mighty strong." Two days out of Egmont, Marie studied the approaching dark clouds warily. "The clouds look scary. Could another cyclone hit so soon?"

"Good question. It could happen." Dad stared into the distance for a few minutes. "Beats me, but I don't like the look of that sky, either. Sure looks threatening."

Silence reigned as we each remembered the recent ordeal. Our survival had been a miracle. The memory was too fresh for any of us to want to face that again.

"Can we escape it somehow?" Claude sat at the tiller, glancing at the sky repeatedly.

"We can't outrun a cyclone." Dad stood, stroking his beard thoughtfully. A sparkle flashed in his eyes. "Then again, maybe we can. I have an idea. If we stay on this course, it'll hit us head on, but what if we turn around and head out of its path?"

"Sounds good to me."

"Let's do it."

Dad took the tiller from Claude. He changed course, hoping to circle around the storm's path and take the long way to our next destination.

The plan worked. We soon found beautiful weather with a nice breeze, the usual trade winds. The sea was relatively calm. The sky was a bright, beautiful blue with not a cloud in sight.

"What's that?" Jolene pointed at something in the distance—something that jumped high out of the water.

At first, I didn't see anything unusual, but then another one jumped.

"Maybe fish swimming in the water." I thought of the tuna we'd caught and its magnificent leaps and twirls. Then I considered the tiny little flying fish that often skipped over the waves. Not realizing our boat was in their path, some regularly landed on our deck.

These creatures weren't just swimming and jumping. The two of them played, enjoying the beautiful weather. Drawing closer, we watched them jump and flip, splashing each other playfully with their fins. Gamboling like a couple of wild kids in a gymnastics class, they weren't fish. They were too big. Much bigger than the tuna we'd caught earlier. Bigger even than our 39-foot long yacht. Jumping in the air, spinning gracefully like ballerinas, the massive creatures didn't have gills like fish. Instead, they had blowholes on their heads.

"Whales!" I cried, happily jumping up and down. "Dad, look at the whales! I didn't know whales played like that."

Dad's expression was grim as he hustled back to the stern. "I'm taking over," he announced brusquely as he wrenched the tiller from Bill.

Bill gave him a puzzled look and shrugged his shoulders. "Guess I'll take a break. Get a bite to eat," he muttered as he headed into the cabin.

"Coming about!" Dad yelled, warning everyone on deck to duck their heads so the heavy boom wouldn't strike them as it swung around. He changed course immediately, without any calculations or planning. Just like that. He ordered more sails up, and we raced away. The whales shrank into the distance.

Every noon, after calculating our position, Dad spent time with his charts, carefully calculating a new course, a course that took into account where we were and where we wanted to go. Dad also considered the effect of the ocean currents and wind in his calculations, but nature rarely acted exactly as expected, so each day a new course was carefully set to our destination.

The helmsman's job was to keep us on course, while keeping an eye out for danger. Changing course to avoid a dangerous storm made sense, but what happened this time? If Bill, a grownup, didn't understand, I certainly wasn't likely to.

I waited until Dad's expression became cheerful once more before asking, "What happened? Why did we leave the whales? I liked watching them have fun."

He glanced back behind us, as though verifying that the whales hadn't followed us.

"Cheryl," he said with a sigh, "the whales were playing with each other. That's true. The problem is they might think the *Berenice* is a playmate and try to play with her. Every year, some ships vanish without a trace. A lot of old salts suspect many are victims of whales who playfully slapped the boats with their powerful tails or flipped onto the ships, expecting them to leap out of the way. The whales don't mean any harm. They're just having fun, but they're so big. They don't realize their own strength. They can easily sink a ship, even one much bigger than us, horsing around like that."

After we'd circled far around the whales, Bill resumed steering toward our next island destination, but we'd entered an ocean current that flowed in the opposite direction. As the wind pushed us one direction and the current pulled the other, the *Berenice* slowed down, almost to a halt. While we barely moved, the ocean around us suddenly came alive.

"Wow! Look at that twirl!" I pointed in the air.

"Hey, that one somersaulted, and this one copied him." Jolene laughed at their antics and applauded the show.

"How do they jump so high?" I wondered, as one flipped in circles before diving down into the water with a huge splash. They were sleek and graceful and sped through the water.

This time, Dad wasn't worried. These porpoises were much smaller than the majestic whales. They wouldn't harm our boat even if they jumped on it or hit it with their tails.

"I've heard stories about porpoises circling a man who's fallen in the water," Dad said, as he watched them with a satisfied smile. "Around and around they'll swim, protecting him. When the sharks charge at him, the porpoises attack back, butting them with their heads until the sharks give up. Porpoises are good creatures to have around."

Flipping, leaping, twirling, somersaulting out of the water, the porpoises put on a lively show. Dozens of them splashed and chirruped all around us. Waving their flippers and nodding their snouts at us, they seemed delighted to see us. We cheered them on. Beautiful and full of fun, they made everyone onboard laugh and smile.

Once their show ended, however, a more somber mood fell. Dad barked more often. Marie and Claude muttered, glared, and found fault with everyone. Bill said nothing but stared morosely. Mom, who rarely complained, muttered as she pulled out the washboard to do laundry. Weeks ago, she found a laundry shortcut. Putting dirty laundry into a mesh market-bag and throwing it overboard, she harnessed the rushing water, using it to pull out all the grime. Now that we were becalmed, her new method didn't work and it was back to the labor-intensive washboard method.

In the distance, several fishing vessels motored past, but even though all our sails were up, we barely moved. Our engine wouldn't start, no matter what Dad tried. At this rate, it would take forever to reach Africa. Despite the fresh fruit from Egmont Island, our food supplies needed replenishing. We caught another tuna, not as big as the last one, and were glad to have it. We had enough food to make it if our journey went as planned, but sitting still in the middle of the Indian Ocean wasn't part of the plan. With the recent detours around the storm and the whales, and now this slowdown from the contrary current, worry crept in. Could we make it?

"What's that?" Jolene pointed toward the stern. The afternoon sun shone brightly. Dad had rigged an awning to give us shade on deck. The sea was calm. A week after leaving Egmont Island, the *Berenice* barely moved.

I squinted to see what she meant. Something flew through the air. "It's not a flying fish," I said as I spied flapping wings. "Hey, I think it's a bird."

"A sparrow!" Dad yelled excitedly, a grin on his face. "Great googa moogas! About time!"

"What's so exciting about a little bird?" I understood enjoying the bird's visit because it made the day more interesting, but Dad seemed overly excited about it.

"Sparrows are land birds. They don't fly far out to sea. This little guy's visit means land's close by."

The jubilation didn't last long. We still sat, barely moving. Land might be near, but it seemed we'd never reach it.

Two days later, on October 24, 1971, we spied land! We made it to Victoria Island, capital of the Seychelles Islands, less than a thousand miles east of Africa. Hurrah!

The relief was short-lived. At the marketplace, the prices were unbelievable.

"You want *how* much for each egg?" Mom asked again, dumbfounded. Surely, she'd heard the man wrong.

He repeated the amount of rupees he wanted. It worked out to about a dollar an egg. Not a dollar for a dozen eggs, but a dollar for just one, single chicken egg. A dozen eggs would cost twelve dollars!

"We can't stock up with prices like this," Mom muttered, turning away from the man's shop and moving on through the marketplace.

It was the same everywhere on the island. Prices were high. Too high. In addition, little was available on this remote island that imported most things from faraway. Perhaps the war in Vietnam made goods scarcer and more expensive in this part of the world. Whatever the reason, we bought only a few supplies before returning to the *Berenice*. A lot fewer than we'd planned.

Dad filled the water tanks with freshwater and made some repairs. Most machines need regular maintenance and repairs to function properly. This was certainly true on a yacht that's constantly exposed to the harmful effects of sun, wind, corrosive saltwater, and constant dampness. Yet our engine needed major work much more often than should be necessary. The engine was fixed again, and after four days, we left Victoria Island. We hoped food would be more readily available and affordable in Durban, South Africa, our next intended port of call.

On the map in my social studies book, it seemed simple enough to sail toward Africa, down through the Mozambique Channel and around to the tip of Africa. Yet there's a reason why explorers such as Christopher Columbus searched for a westward route from Europe to Asia, a route that avoided sailing around Africa. Some of the most treacherous sailing on Earth happens around Africa. We were about to discover for ourselves just how difficult sailing around Africa can be.

19. Engine? What Engine?

Nov. 2, 1971

"Blasted engine!" Dad slammed tools down as he tried to fix the engine. Again. A hopeful roar was followed by a gurgle and a whine, and the engine gave up the ghost.

"That does it! Overhauled this piece of rubbish seven times! Seven times! Wasted too much time and money for nothing!" he growled at no one in particular. Thwack! He hit it with the spanner, the monkey wrench, one more time. "Stupid battery's leaking. Eating a hole in the hull! Useless piece of junk!"

Dad later wrote in his terse log that he "effected repairs." In other words, he patched the damaged hull with quick-drying cement, and he got rid of the engine problem. He actually got rid of it completely. Somehow, Dad tossed the motor overboard, to protect the *Berenice*'s hull from further damage. Now the engine wouldn't give us any more trouble. It wouldn't cost any more money. Then again, we'd have no electricity. There'd be no refrigeration, ever. No electric lights for emergencies. No radio in case of trouble. No motor to ease our way through harbors and other tight spots.

It wasn't as though we used those things often. Sails powered our yacht most of the time, especially since the engine rarely functioned properly. We rarely used the refrigerator, eating everything served at a meal so there were no leftovers to refrigerate. We ate mostly canned or other nonperishable foods or, when we could get them, fresh fruits and vegetables that didn't require refrigeration. We went to bed when the sun sank and got up in the morning as it rose. Our kerosene lanterns would still work in emergencies. We didn't have a television; for entertainment, we told stories, sang songs, or watched nature. Our life was more relaxed without electricity, so we sailed on, without an engine.

Bill brought out the fishing line again. The mackerel he landed wasn't nearly as large as the first tuna, but fresh fish made a nice change to our diet and stretched our diminishing supplies further. We passed through excellent fishing grounds where we caught another delicious fish the next day, and observed numerous Japanese fishing boats in the distance. Mom pointed to several of their floating green glass balls as we sailed past some of their fishing nets.

Heading south, we skirted the coast of northeastern Africa. Most of the time, the coast was just over the horizon, but sometimes, we were close enough to catch a glimpse of Africa. Occasionally, we saw it in the distance as a long low shadowy cloud on the horizon, but other times we sailed so near we could make out the rocky coastline and its cliffs.

We did not attempt to sail into a harbor here. This area was a place to bypass quickly, if possible, not a place to go ashore. For hundreds—perhaps thousands—of years, pirates roamed these waters unchecked. These weren't storybook pirates who dressed like Captain Hook and his crew. They might not wear eye patches, pantaloons, or wooden legs, but they were pirates nonetheless. This sort snuck up in swift boats and tried to steal everything onboard. They might even snatch the entire boat. Some would hold people for ransom, sell them as slaves, or even commit murder. These weren't romantic Disney pirates but dangerous criminals. This was definitely not a place to go ashore.

Dad kept a rifle ready, just in case. If necessary, he'd shoot anyone who tried to come onboard without permission. The law of the sea gave him that right, but he'd rather avoid trouble if possible. We kept out of sight of the coast as much as possible. We wouldn't land until we reached more civilized countries in southern Africa.

The weather seemed to be on our side as a strong southeasterly wind pushed us at a nice clip for several days. Then, it turned on us. Literally. The wind now pushed us back in the opposite direction, back over the stretch of ocean we'd just traveled, deeper into the heart of the dangerous region we wanted to avoid.

Thankfully, a few days later, the wind changed again and we sailed southward over the same stretch of ocean for the third time. Without a motor, we were at the mercy of fickle winds that couldn't seem to decide which direction to blow. Too scared to find a harbor, we could only go where the wind pushed us.

Abruptly, the wind died. Just quit entirely. The *Berenice* couldn't move at all, so we just sat there.

"Wally," Mom called to my dad as we sat becalmed. "Could you come take a look at this?"

"What's wrong?" he asked, seeing the worried expression on her face.

The crew was on deck enjoying the calm, sunny weather, but Mom lowered her voice and looked around to make sure none of the crew could overhear. She lifted the sheet of plywood that supported the berth's mattress and doubled as a lid to the storage area underneath. "Look," she said, pointing into the storage area.

Dad bent over to peer into the dark region where our food was stored. He stroked the dark brown beard he'd grown during the trip since shaving was difficult at sea. Razors quickly rusted in the salt air. Saltwater stung and irritated a freshly shaven face. Besides, shaving on a rocking vessel could be dangerous. A sudden gust of wind or a large wave hitting the side of the ship could make a man jerk and seriously cut himself.

Standing straight, he looked at Mom and shrugged his shoulders. "Not much in there to see," he said.

Mom nodded. "Our supplies are running seriously low," she said gravely. "There's not much left. We'll be out of food soon."

After a moment of silence, Dad grimly said, "Carolyn, we've got a worse problem. The freshwater tanks are almost empty. If we don't reach a safe harbor soon, we'll be out of water."

People can survive without food for weeks, but not without water. Few people survive more than three days without potable water. Though ocean water surrounded us, we couldn't get drinkable water from the sea. Mom carefully conserved water, even mixing seawater and freshwater in her cooking when a recipe required water and salt, but our freshwater tanks were dangerously low.

"Dad, why can't people drink seawater?" I asked later that day.

"Someone's been listening to other people's conversations; huh?" He mussed my blonde hair with his hand, a smile on his lips but a serious look in his eyes. "Well, Pumpkin, if someone drinks seawater, the salt in it makes him thirstier, instead of quenching his thirst."

"Can't he just drink more saltwater?" I asked.

"No, too much saltwater will make him sick. Even make him crazy. Or kill him. It's better to drink a tiny bit of freshwater than lots of saltwater. We just need to be careful not to waste our freshwater," he reassured me, and with a sigh, he plodded off to work on cleaning some equipment.

There always seemed to be plenty of work to do onboard a ship to keep it running smoothly.

The wind seemed to play an evil game with us. First, it pushed us one direction. Then it flipped around and pushed us the opposite direction, making us retrace the path we'd just traveled. We made little headway, seemed no closer to refilling our freshwater tanks or restocking our food supplies.

As the situation grew worse, tempers grew shorter. It had been three weeks since we last visited a harbor. Three weeks since anyone had a chance to be alone. It wouldn't take much to start trouble now.

"Mom, Pear-Paw's at it again!" I screamed one sultry afternoon. "He threw more toys overboard! We won't have any left!"

Jolene sobbed, while Pierre-Paul stood nearby wearing a devilish grin. His mom lay on the other side of the deck in her bathing suit. With her eyes closed, she worked on perfecting her suntan and ignored the commotion, as usual.

"That's it!" Mom roared, as she marched over to where the three of us stood peering into the water below, looking for some sign of the toys he'd deep-sixed. "I can't take this anymore! This has gone on too long. If you won't do anything about his behavior, I guess I'll have to." She turned and glared at Marie, but Marie just rolled from her back to her stomach.

Grabbing Pierre-Paul by one arm, Mom plunked herself down on the cabin. She spun him around, and before he knew what had happened, she put him over her knee and gave him a couple of swift, forceful swats with her hand. Setting him on his feet again, Mom waved her finger near his face as she thundered, "Pierre-Paul! You do not throw other people's things into the ocean. Do you understand me? You do not take anything that belongs to someone else. Ever!" She gave him that look, the one all mothers seem to have, the look that warned him not to mess with her again.

Pierre-Paul didn't say a word. He rubbed his bottom gently with one hand. His grin was gone. His eyes were as big as golf balls. No one had ever spoken sternly to him before, let alone spanked him. He was clearly shocked, but he didn't destroy any more of our belongings. No more toys or books disappeared down the bilge. No more toys were thrown overboard.

From that moment on, Pierre-Paul was a different child. Well, around my mom anyway. He immediately did anything she asked. He no longer ordered her about, as he did his own parents. If Mom gave him the slightest look, he immediately stopped any misbehavior.

Mom's action made life better for Jolene and me. We weren't constantly on guard, protecting our few belongings, but Marie didn't take the punishment nearly as well as he had.

"How dare you put a hand on my son!" she screamed, jumping up from the deck. Her eyes seemed on fire as she came at my mother.

Marie didn't realize the magnitude of her son's bad behavior. She didn't understand the enormity of theft and destruction out at sea where people's belongings can't be replaced easily. In centuries past, a sailor caught stealing had a hand cut off. Some were even keelhauled, a punishment few survived.

A criminal who was keelhauled was tied with a rope and thrown overboard. Using the rope, other sailors dragged the miscreant under the ship, across the keel at the bottom of the ship's hull, and up the other side of the boat. If they pulled fast enough, and he held his breath long enough, he wouldn't drown, but the barnacles, sharp little shellfish that attach themselves to the bottom of most ships, would slice his clothing and skin. Barnacles are dirty creatures, so the cuts would likely become infected. Many didn't survive keelhauling, so most old-time sailors knew better than to touch someone else's belongings.

However, Marie didn't know that. She didn't understand that her refusal to address the problem left Mom no choice but to handle the situation herself. She didn't realize that Mom had been patient far longer than most would have been. She only knew that Mom hurt her child.

Marie ran at Mom, her fists pulled back, ready to attack. Dad and Claude came running. Together they stepped between the women and managed to prevent a fistfight.

Our problems with Pierre-Paul were over. He wouldn't take any more of our things, but now we had a bigger problem. Marie and Mom were angry at each other.

Mom was mad that Marie had refused to control her own child. That Marie had let her son bully us and destroy so many things. That she hadn't tried to intervene. Even more, Mom was mad that Marie had forced Mom to break her own code of ethics and interfere with someone else's child. Of course, Marie's yelling and threatening to strike Mom didn't help either.

Marie, on the other hand, would not forgive Mom for striking her son, or for speaking to him so sternly, so roughly. Marie glared at Mom, day after day. Whenever she looked at Mom, Marie's mouth pursed, her brow furrowed, and her fists clenched. Clearly, Marie was not giving up the fight.

On a small ketch, far out at sea, there's little privacy. There's no place to get away and cool off. There's no way to avoid someone else, and no way this could end well.

20. Good-bye, Pierre-Paul!

Nov. 9, 1971

A couple of days later, Claude took his turn at the helm. Since the spanking, he kept Marie by his side as much as possible, hoping to avoid a physical fight. Marie sat on the aft cabin with her arms folded across her chest, her eyes narrowed, and her chin jutted forward. When she spoke, she spat the words at Claude, often softly enough that we couldn't make out the words, though her angry tone was impossible to miss.

Bill hovered near them. His syrupy voice was soft, too, but he didn't seem to be speaking words of peace, since Marie and Claude grew stiffer as he spoke. Claude glared at the compass as he manned the tiller and said nothing.

Down below, Mom and Dad whispered, too. "Have you noticed the case of candy?" Mom asked.

"No, what's the matter with it?" Dad hadn't joked in days. The strain caused by the feud, the threat of pirates, and the constant fight against the elements left him looking weary, with dark bags under his brown eyes, and a fire in his eyes that hinted that his temper smoldered and might explode at any moment.

"It's disappearing."

"Well, it's meant to be eaten. Maybe the kids have been into it." Dad sighed and slowly shook his head.

"No one eats that much candy without getting sick. The kids can't reach that high. If they somehow climbed up, they'd dump the box trying to get the M&Ms out," Mom insisted. She opened the cardboard box to show Dad what remained.

"I think someone's hoarding candy," Mom added. She nodded in the direction of the crew. Hoarding food, stockpiling it to get more than your fair share, is a serious crime at sea, especially when supplies are low. Hoarding food at sea is as serious as stealing or maybe worse, since lives are at stake.

Dad glowered at the cabin doorway. "Can't be Bill," Dad decided. "His belongings are stored right here in the galley, out in the open. We'd notice if he took things."

Mom nodded. "Right." She raised her eyebrows and nodded her head repeatedly toward the forward cabin.

"But we don't have proof. We can't be certain . . ." Dad cupped one hand over the other and let out a long breath. "On the other hand, there's no other reasonable explanation. At least, none I can think of."

"What should we do?" Mom asked.

"I'm not sure, but we can't go on like this. I'm going ask them to leave at the next port. We don't have money to pay their passage to Durban, but we'll figure out something if we have to. It was bad enough when it just involved the kids."

They looked over at me. I sat on a nearby berth, reading the Australian classic *Snugglepot and Cuddlepie* about tiny gum nut creatures and their adventures as they hoped to see humans. I looked back at the text and pretended to be oblivious to their conversation.

They lowered their voices further. I heard something about lies. Lots of lies. I wasn't sure what the lies were, but no one wants to live in close quarters with people you can't trust.

Sailing down the Mozambique Channel, between the large island of Madagascar and Mozambique on the southeastern coast of Africa, our fight against contrary winds continued. We made headway for a while, only to be blown back, and then have to repeat the same journey again. Forward and back. Forward and back. For twelve days, we traversed the same patch of water. We seemed to make little or no progress.

Occasionally we saw other vessels out at sea. Mostly, we saw oil tankers or other large ships in the distance, traveling the shipping lanes, the routes the big ships favored. Sometimes, fishing boats crossed our path briefly. Less often, we saw yachts and other pleasure craft cruising along. On the rare occasions when we passed close enough to make out the people onboard, we waved.

This time, though, a vessel didn't remain in the distance. A fishing boat turned toward us and came closer and closer until it was close enough to hear the captain yell a greeting.

"Need help?" he asked. "Want a tow?" He pointed to a rope he could throw to us, in case we didn't understand his English.

"That'd be great, mate!" Dad hollered back. He grabbed the line tossed and wrapped it around a cleat, in figure-eight fashion, until he was satisfied that the rope was secure. Then he gave a thumbs-up signal to the fisherman indicating that we were ready.

Soon we were safely moored in Antonio Enes, a city in Mozambique later renamed Angoche. The fisherman said he'd noticed our yacht one day and paid scant attention to it, but then he saw us again the next day. And the next. And the next. He'd heard many stories of woe about the stretch of water that surrounded his home. Guessing we must be in trouble, our Good Samaritan came to our rescue.

Dad thanked him repeatedly for his help, for towing us ashore, but he waved off our gratitude saying he hoped someone would do the same thing for him if he ever needed help. Nevertheless, he was our hero.

As soon as we anchored in the harbor, Claude signaled a water taxi. Our entire crew climbed into the small motor boat. As usual, they planned to go sightseeing.

The moment the water taxi was out of sight, Mom and Dad jumped into action. In the forward cabin, they grabbed Claude and Marie's bags. Emptying the storage areas, they stuffed the couple's belongings into their bags. Hoards of M&Ms and other supplies were uncovered. There was no doubt now. Dad carted the bags to the cockpit, and then they packed Bill's bags, too.

A couple of hours later, the water taxi returned. A pile of bags sat on our deck in plain sight. Dad stood nearby. The water taxi's engine grew quieter as it pulled alongside the *Berenice*. Claude scrambled to the deck of the water taxi, but before he could touch our vessel, Dad held up his hand.

"Stop where you are," Dad ordered, glaring icily. Waving his hands at the bags, he added, "We packed your bags for you. I'll toss them to you. No reason for you to come aboard."

"Hmmph. We only came to get our gear," Claude sneered, as he got into position, ready to catch the first bag.

One piece at a time, Dad tossed their luggage to them. The water taxi turned and headed back to shore. We were glad to see them go, glad to be rid of the tension and trouble, and so glad to have some privacy and peace again.

For the first time since leaving Darwin three months earlier, there were only five of us onboard the *Berenice*. The crew gone, only our family remained. After a few days, Dad found a fellow named Gustos who wanted to sail to South Africa with us, but he didn't have a passport. We didn't want to wait a month, or more, for him to get the necessary papers. Dad wanted out of here, away from our old crew, as soon as possible. Besides, we needed to get to a town that wasn't so poor, in a country without the violence of a civil war, where we could actually stock up on supplies. We couldn't stay here long.

"We've sailed over 5,000 miles in the past five months. Gained a lot of experience. Made it safely through a cyclone. I think we can make it to South Africa without a crew." Dad tried to convince Mom. "Joshua Slocum sailed around the world by himself. We'll have twice the sailors he had."

Mom sighed. "Well, we could certainly do without the problems crews have created," she agreed. "They've eaten more than we planned, leaving us short of food. Some haven't done their fair share of work, thinking they were on vacation. To say nothing of the lying and stealing we endured. I think we made a big mistake, not making them pay for their food."

They decided to go on, without a crew, at least for now.

"Okay, girls. Want to move into the forward cabin?" Dad asked.

"Yes!" we cheered, jumping up and down.

Jolene and I would have a room of our own. We wouldn't have to sleep in the galley anymore. We'd have a place to play that wasn't in the walkway. We wouldn't have to worry about people stepping on us. We wouldn't have to move our things whenever someone wanted to sit for a minute. We could leave our belongings on our beds during mealtimes. I would have a room of my own. Well, I'd have a room to share with Jolene, that is.

I was glad the crew was gone. Even though Pierre-Paul had quit destroying our things, he rarely played with us. He was rude and mean and didn't like our games. We'd have a much better time without him.

However, we would have extra work now. Dad said we were still too young to help sail the *Berenice*, but we'd take over some chores Mom previously did. I would take care of my sisters more often. I'd feed five-month-old Jackie and change her diapers, watch over her and entertain her while Mom was busy. Jackie was growing more alert and didn't sleep constantly anymore. I'd be in charge of Jolene, too, when Mom and Dad were busy. Mostly that meant that I had to keep her out of their way.

Mom and Dad would bear the brunt of the burden. They would sleep less and work harder. The two of them would do all the work five adults had done—work that had sometimes kept five adults busy. We'd make it without a crew. We hoped.

21. HARVEY

Day or night, someone had to steer the *Berenice*. Someone had to make sure we stayed on course. Without a crew, Mom and Dad took turns steering, all day and all night. When one finished a four-hour watch, the other took over. Neither could sleep more than four hours at a stretch.

However, one afternoon that changed. Dad excitedly called us up on deck to see something. Everyone came running. That is, everyone ran except Jackie. She would soon be six months old and wasn't even crawling yet.

What was the excitement about? Nothing looked different. There was no land in sight. No animals were visible nearby. Nothing on the boat looked different, but Dad stood on the deck, arms crossed, with a grin across his bearded face.

Mom stifled a yawn. She stared at Dad, turned to look at the cockpit, and then turned back to look at Dad again. "Wally," she asked, "If you're standing here, who's steering?"

The boat wasn't behaving the way we expected it to without a helmsman. It didn't suddenly turn another direction. The sails didn't flap or the boom waffle. Instead, she sailed smoothly along.

"Harvey." That was Dad's answer. Just that. "Harvey."

"Who's Harvey?" I asked.

"He's an invisible, six-foot-tall, white rabbit." He said it with a straight face, but a telltale sparkle lit his eyes.

"There aren't any rabbits out here," Jolene argued.

"Rabbits aren't invisible. Or six feet tall," I added.

What was Dad up to? Eventually he explained. First, he described an old movie called "Harvey." A famous actor, Jimmy Stewart, played a man who claimed to have an invisible white rabbit as a friend. His family thought he was crazy, but at the end of the movie, a psychiatrist discovered Harvey was real.

Then he explained that sometimes a yacht is perfectly balanced. No one understood how it happened, but sometimes it did. It couldn't be planned. It just happened.

Why would that be a big deal? Well, a perfectly balanced boat, when pointed in a certain direction, will continue to head in that direction by itself—without anyone steering it. As long as no sudden gusts of wind or huge waves knock it, the boat will stay on course.

Dad suspected the *Berenice* was one of those rare yachts, and he'd been testing his theory. He lashed a bungee cord to the tiller, with the other end secured around a railing post at the deck's edge. The cord was a safety precaution to prevent sudden unexpected gusts from capsizing her.

"But it's working! It's really working," he said excitedly. He pointed at the compass. "See! We're still on the course I set hours ago. Do you know what this means?" His eyes grew wide as he bounced in place.

I shook my head. What was so exciting about a boat steering herself?

"Don't you see? What a difference this will make! We can take breaks from steering! If the weather's fairly decent and we're far from any known dangers, Harvey . . ." He stopped and pointed dramatically at the tiller as though an invisible creature really sat there steering the boat. "Harvey can take the watch. And your mother and I can sleep." He folded his arms and nodded his head, a satisfied smile on his lips.

Mom and Dad wouldn't have to stay up half the night, every night. Instead, Harvey took the night watches. The adults still checked on Harvey periodically to make sure he was doing his job, but good old faithful Harvey was always there, keeping us right on course. Harvey not only gave the adults more rest. Now, we could all eat meals together, something we hadn't done since the crew left. Maybe, with Harvey's help, we could make it without a crew.

22. Stop! Don't Run Us Over!

"Batten down the hatches! Trim the sails!" Dad yelled, as a terrific gust of wind hit, sending lines flying and slicing through the mizzen.

Mom ran about the deck. Together, they lowered several sails before the wind ripped any more. They secured everything loose as they began the fight with another gale.

A while later, Dad shook his fist at the wind and threw his sail repair kit through the cabin doorway. "I give up! Put that away."

Mom looked up from where she sat checking my lessons. "Did you fix the sail?" she asked hopefully. She picked up the repair kit from where it landed, and put it away. She poured him a cup of hot coffee.

"No," Dad said fiercely. "Wind's too strong. Can't repair any more sails until the weather calms down. Callen's Sail Repair Shop is closed for now. I've got to get back." He gulped down the drink and handed her the empty cup. Harvey couldn't be trusted to handle a storm, so Dad had to hurry back to the helm.

The next day, the wind calmed a little, but only a little. With just one small sail up, the *Berenice* raced along.

"A ship!" Mom pointed. She sat at the tiller, taking her turn on watch.

We occasionally saw ships in the distance, but this one was different. Instead of continuing on its course, the ship turned and headed in our direction. After a few minutes, it turned back to its former path. That was odd. Why did it change course twice?

A little while later, another huge ship did the same thing. And then another.

"What's with the ships today?" I asked Dad, as he sat at his navigation desk, eating a snack while checking his charts. The huge maps included lots of information needed by sailors such as how deep the water was, where rocks or sunken ships or other hidden dangers lay, and where channels of deeper water offered safe passage.

"What do you mean?" he asked, looking up.

"Another ship moved closer to us and then went back. Why are they doing that?"

"Hmm, probably checking on us, making sure we aren't in trouble from the storm," Dad suggested. He moved to the porthole to look.

It was comforting to think that the big ships were watching over a little boat like ours. That they were ready to rescue us if need be.

Through the porthole, something else caught our attention. A school of dolphins swam by. We'd seen many dolphins, but these were unusual.

"Hey, look, their bellies are pink!" I giggled.

"Huh? Wonder what that means?" Dad asked.

I shrugged and stared at them for a few minutes before returning to play with the baby. She was old enough now to enjoy games such as "This Little Piggy." I enjoyed caring for her, even if it meant changing a stinky diaper occasionally.

Though I didn't say anything, I had noticed that only a few tins of baby formula remained. What would happen to Jackie if we ran out? She could eat mashed bananas or other fresh fruit if we had them, but she was too little to eat much else. Worse yet, our freshwater supply was dangerously low again. If we ran out of formula or drinkable water, the baby would be in big trouble.

When the storm passed, Mom baked a cake to celebrate both making it through the storm without a crew and finally getting the genoa repaired. The celebration was short-lived. When Dad calculated our position, he discovered we'd been blown back quite a distance by the storm. We'd have to retrace our path again.

All down the coast of Africa, we fought the wind. Sailing through the Mozambique Channel, on our way to South Africa, several gales hit. One storm stopped only for another to strike. Whenever we made progress, a storm blew us back. Plus, the wind strength kept changing. The wind would weaken, and Mom and Dad would raise more sails—or sheets as Dad called them—so we could make progress. A little while later, the wind would pick up speed, and my parents would race to lower several sheets, so the Berenice wouldn't race dangerously fast and the sails wouldn't tear. Raising and lowering sails was hard, exhausting work.

Dad grew mad easily—very easily. Mom was quiet—very quiet.

"At this rate, we won't reach South Africa until next year!" Dad slammed his fist against the navigation table after calculating our position. Once again, the *Berenice* had lost ground.

November twenty-eighth began well. The weather was fair for a change. We made great progress toward Durban with a nice steady breeze, under a cloudless, blue sky. Yet the afternoon was about to turn grim.

A ship, a massive tanker as big as a city, headed in our direction. Unlike previous ones, this ship didn't turn back to the usual shipping channels after a few minutes. It hadn't made a quick detour to check on us. Instead, it charged toward us. Closer and closer it came, with no sign of changing its course.

"I think it's heading toward us," Mom said worriedly. "Wally, I don't think its captain realizes we're here."

Dad had told stories about massive ships finding sails, masts, and other pieces of yachts stuck to their hulls as silent evidence of a boat destroyed because the giant never saw the miniscule vessel in its path. Huge ships were supposed to steer clear of smaller vessels that couldn't move as fast, but a monster's helmsman was so far above the water that unless he was constantly alert, he could easily fail to notice small vessels like ours.

"We need to get out of here fast." Dad jerked the tiller, steering out of the tanker's path. "Carolyn, we're coming about."

Mom ran to adjust the sails. Together, they frantically worked on our escape. The ship seemed to grow larger every second, as it sped ever closer.

Suddenly, our sails flapped uselessly. The approaching ship now blocked our wind. We couldn't move. Without a motor, we were stranded in the path of this oncoming monster.

"Hey, we're here! Stop! Turn around!"

"Stop! Turn the ship! Don't run us over!"

Mom and Dad jumped up and down. Waving their arms vigorously over their heads, they screamed at the top of their lungs. Desperately they tried to get the attention of people on the oil tanker to let them know we were down here and would be run over unless they quickly changed course.

The ship kept coming. She seemed wider than several houses now and taller than any house I'd ever seen, yet she kept growing larger. No one onboard seemed to notice my parents' antics. What else could we do?

"I'll get the flare gun. You keep trying to get their attention," Dad yelled at Mom as he scrambled into the aft cabin. A minute later, he popped up with the signal gun. Aiming high, he shot into the air near the ship's navigation deck. High in the air, the flare exploded like a brilliant fireworks display, but it was designed to attract help in the dark. The flare was hard to see in the bright glare of the afternoon sun. No one on the humungous ship seemed to notice it.

The huge gray metallic monster sped onward. The ship had too many decks to count with one stacked above another. Even the lowest deck towered above us, higher than a multi-story building, far, far above the surface of the water. Its engines drowned out the sounds of the wind and waves.

"Everybody on deck, now!" Dad yelled, in a tone that brooked no nonsense. "To the stern immediately," he growled, pointing at the end of our yacht farthest from the oncoming ship.

Though the roar of the huge engines made it hard to hear anything, Dad's words were clear. I grabbed Jackie and hurried to the stern. Mom, her face as pale as our white sails, took six-month-old Jackie from my arms. Mom said nothing. Jolene and I stood quietly, staring at the large gray monster that grew closer by the moment. The ship now seemed large enough to swallow more than a block of houses. I felt like a bug staring up at an elephant. Would the elephant notice the bug?

"When I say, 'Jump,' everybody jumps over the side. Swim as far and as fast as you can. Away from that ship. Understand?" Dad hollered, even though he stood next to us.

I nodded solemnly. So did Mom and Jolene. None of us made a sound. Even baby Jackie was silent. My body shook. I didn't see how I could possibly swim faster than that huge, speeding ship. I didn't want to jump into the ocean with sharks and other creatures waiting below. I didn't want to get separated from Mom and Dad, but I stood there, silently, waiting for the order.

Darkness fell as the ship loomed over us, blocking most of the sunlight. It was so near; it towered above us. I felt the heat given off by its metallic hull and saw the rivets that held the huge plates of steel together. Grease and oil fumes filled the air. We leaned over the rail, ready to jump on command.

Suddenly, the huge tanker seemed to slow down. No, it hadn't slowed down. It only seemed to. Was it? Yes, it was! It was turning. It was so big and so fast. Yet somehow, incredibly, it made a turn tighter than an eighteen-wheeler on a highway could have made. It was impossible to make such a huge ship turn so suddenly, but we'd seen it with our own eyes. We hugged each other as the ship's side came into view.

"Why did you wait so long to say, 'Jump!'?" Mom asked as the tanker receded into the distance. "Did you know it was turning?"

"No," Dad said quietly, his face an ashen gray. His shoulders slumped. He sighed and shook his head. "No one could swim fast enough to get away from it. I knew it was a death sentence. I couldn't give the order."

That night we gave heart-felt prayers of thanksgiving for our miraculous rescue.

23. Climbing the Walls

The next afternoon, after a day of little progress, we spied the lighthouse off Bazaruto Island. The lighthouse warned of dangers to ships, but it also announced a safe port was close by. If only we could maneuver around the hazards, we could soon anchor at Inhambane, Mozambique.

To sail into the harbor, we first had to get past the Barra Point sand bar. Without an engine and with the wind against us, this wouldn't be easy. We tacked, zigzagging back and forth, back and forth, aiming for the small break in the sand bar where the water was deep enough to sail through. The wind wouldn't cooperate. We turned around and sailed back some distance, like a pitcher returning to the mound to take aim again before throwing the ball. Again, the wind pushed us right to the sand bar itself. The hill of sand could rip the hull out if the *Berenice* rammed into it. Again and again, we tried, but we didn't make it over that day.

All night long, Dad tacked in front of the sand bar. As dawn arrived, the wind and tide finally cooperated enough and we sailed past the bar that had blocked our path. Several hours later, we finally reached anchorage.

The port captain's boat motored out to meet the *Berenice* in the harbor. He came onboard to check our passports, make sure we weren't carrying anything illegal, and fill out forms. The doctor who came with him checked our shot records and gave a quick medical exam to make sure we weren't bringing any terrible diseases. Down in the galley, the port captain looked around curiously. When he spotted six-month-old Jackie, he made silly faces and cooed. He chatted easily with Dad.

Handing back our passports, he turned to me with a big smile. Crouching down slightly, he looked me in the eye. "Well, someone has a birthday this week. How old will you be?"

"Seven. I'll be seven years old," I answered proudly.

"Happy birthday." Turning to Mom, he added, "You should meet my wife. She speaks a little English. She'd love to help you pick up some supplies, though there isn't much in Inhambane's market. You'll have to stock up at the next port," he said apologetically.

"Oh, I wouldn't want to bother her," Mom replied.

"Nonsense, she'll love it. Give her a chance to practice her English," he insisted.

After the shopping trip, his wife entertained Mom and us children in their home, while Dad filled the water tanks and took care of other business. Then the lovely lady insisted the men join us for dinner. What a delicious meal. Fresh fruits and vegetables tasted heavenly after living so long on canned foods.

As the meal ended, our hostess rose from her table. Mom tried to get up and help clear the table, but the lady waved her hand, signaling for everyone else to stay seated. The twinkle in her eyes and broad smile across her face hinted that she was up to something. Over at the kitchen counter, with her back to us, she fussed about for a couple of minutes. When she turned around, she held a cake with seven lit candles on top. Her husband broke into a hearty chorus of "Happy Birthday," and my family quickly joined in.

"Oh!" I cried, with a gasp. A surprise birthday party! Remembering my manners, and the touch of Portuguese I'd learned, I thanked them for the party. "Obrigado!"

Though their country was in the midst of civil war, the port captain was the friendliest official we'd ever met. That's saying a lot since many officials around the world invited us to tea or escorted us on a tour of their town. Perhaps his friendliness wasn't despite the war. Maybe because there was no peace here, he and his wife worked hard to bring as much peace and civility into their own lives as they could.

As the port captain predicted, there weren't many goods for sale in the market. At least we stocked up on formula for Jackie, and the freshwater tanks were full once more. After resting for a couple of days, we were ready to continue the journey. We were anxious to reach Durban in South Africa where supplies would be plentiful.

Sailing out of the harbor, heading towards the sea, we approached the sand bar that had given us so much trouble a few days earlier. As the *Berenice* approached, the wind died down. Then it changed direction. Without an engine, getting past the sand bar was tricky. Very tricky. After trying most of the day without success, Dad finally gave up for the night.

We sailed back into the harbor, out of the channel, so other vessels wouldn't collide with us, and anchored in a safe spot for the night. He planned to try again when the sun rose, so we went to bed for the night.

Bump!

Something jolted me awake during the night. I sat up and tried to figure out what had happened. I peered into the darkness. Dimly, I made out shapes. Something was wrong, but I wasn't sure what. I scrambled off my bunk. Hmm, I must be dreaming. The furniture had moved, but that was impossible. It's all built in and bolted down. So what had happened? As I moved across the tiny triangular-shaped room, nothing was where it should be. Slowly, I realized I wasn't walking on the floor. The floor was over there, going up like a wall. Instead, I walked across the concrete wall at the side of my bed. I crossed the wall like a spider! Then I climbed the bulkhead, the wall at the end of the bed, in order to reach the doorway. This must be a crazy, mixed-up dream.

"Cheryl, is that you?"

I heard Mom's voice, but I couldn't see her through the darkness.

"Yes," I said slowly. I listened, trying to figure out where she was.

"Are you all right?"

I clambered toward the sound of her voice. Entering the galley, I could see much better.

There were no portholes in our forward bedroom. An overhead hatch could let in sunshine and a breeze during fair weather, but it was securely closed at night to keep out malaria-carrying mosquitoes. Since first landing in Africa, we took quinine pills daily and did everything else we could to avoid malaria, a disease that caused fever, headaches, and sometimes death. Malaria was a serious problem in this part of the world.

Here in the main cabin, glass-covered portholes let in light without worry of mosquitoes. The moon and stars provided enough light through the portholes for me to see, but even the light seemed odd. Then I realized the light only came through the portholes on one side of the cabin.

I rubbed my eyes. I couldn't believe what I saw. This had to be a dream.

Mom sat on a wall. Not on top of a wall, instead she sat on the side of the wall. The floor and ceiling were parallel to her body, as though gravity no longer existed.

"I guess I'm okay. What happened?" I yawned as I made my way over to where she sat holding the six-month-old.

"A storm hit during the night. Picked us up, anchor and all, and moved us. We're practically on the beach. The water's too shallow here, so the *Berenice* has fallen onto her side."

Well, that explained walking on the walls.

After a while, a dark shadow appeared in the cabin doorway.

"Throttle handle's missing. It broke off. Doesn't seem to be any other damage," Dad said. "Not much we can do now. Just wait for the tide to come in and hope the water will be deep enough to float us out to deeper water." He looked around. "Where's Jolene?"

I shrugged. "Still asleep, I guess."

Mom handed Jackie to me. Then she climbed into our room to check on Jolene. Jolene's berth was on the side of the boat that now rose into the air. Gravity had dumped her from the vertical berth, despite the leeboard, and she lay on the opposite side of the room, where she must have landed. But she was sound asleep.

Jolene had a reputation as a sound sleeper. One morning back in Australia, when she was very little, I awoke to find her bed empty. She wasn't in our bedroom. She wasn't in the living room or in the kitchen. She wasn't in the water closet, as we called the bathroom. Where was she?

I asked Mom what had happened, and Mom and Dad frantically searched the small brick house from one end to the other. She wasn't under the bed. She wasn't in any of her favorite hide-and-seek spots. Where was she?

Dad went to the hall closet to grab his jacket, ready launch a neighborhood search, but there, on the floor of the closet, was Jolene. Curled in a ball, she was fast asleep. She must have walked there in her sleep, shut the door on herself, and dozed again. None of our frantic yells had woken her.

Over time, we learned it was practically impossible to wake Jolene if she wasn't ready to wake up. But this was incredible! How could she fall off her comfortable bed onto a cold, damp concrete wall several feet away, without waking up? Yet, there she was, sleeping soundly, and after a brief discussion, Mom and Dad decided to let her sleep.

That mystery solved, Dad went back on deck. Well, actually, he walked across the cabin walls not the deck. He shot a flare into the air, trying to get help. Mom and I waited, talking quietly in the galley, as baby Jackie slept in Mom's arms.

We sat in the dark. Uncomfortable on the cold concrete wall, time passed slowly. Eventually, dawn's rosy glow lit the cabin. The tide began to rise. Slowly, the *Berenice* lifted. Gradually, it tilted back into an upright position. We were afloat again! We sailed back into deeper water in the dim light of the wee hours of the morning and dropped anchor. Safe and secure once more, we went back to bed, exhausted.

When I awoke later that morning, I had a lot to tell my little sister. "Guess what? We were blown onto the beach last night. The whole boat tipped over. We walked on the walls, like bugs!"

She rolled her eyes at me in disbelief. When Mom backed up my story, she petulantly asked, "Why didn't you wake me? I missed all the fun."

Mom and I looked at each other. I rolled my eyes, and we both burst into laughter. Even being tossed onto cement hadn't woken her. How did she expect us to wake her?

24. The Power of Prayer

Once again, we attempted to sail past the sand bar that blocked our way to the sea. All day, we tried to reach the narrow section that was deep enough for us to pass over, but we fought both the tide and the wind. When the water was deep enough to sail over a section of the sand bar, the wind was against us; maneuver as he might, Dad couldn't sail the *Berenice* to the exact spot needed. When the wind changed in our favor, the tide was out and the water was too shallow for us to get past the bar.

Dad muttered and slammed things about. With his jaw clenched, he looked ready to explode. I stayed out of his way.

As darkness fell, Dad muttered, "That's it! I won't turn back again! I refuse to face this same blasted sand bar another day."

"Wally," Mom said, trying to be the voice of reason, "We can't stay in the channel. A ship could hit us in the dark."

"Grrr," Dad growled. He paced the deck. He stared at the sand bar. Then he stuck his index finger in his mouth. Pulling the wet finger out and holding it high in the air, he tested the wind direction again. He dropped a weighted rope over the side, until the weight hit the sand at the bottom of the channel. Pulling up the rope, he measured the length that was wet.

"Water's not quite deep enough, but the tide's moving in our favor. At this rate, we can sail over soon." Dad paced the deck, stroking his beard. Then he stopped and announced, "I am going to wait right here. I think we can do it tonight."

Mom looked skeptically at the stars that dotted the sky. She squinted across the water at the channel markers that were getting hard to see in the fading light. Then she turned to look at Dad, with a raised eyebrow, but she didn't say a word.

"We're going to do it tonight. If humanly possible," Dad repeated.

Half an hour later, Dad yelled, "Cheryl, get up on the port side." He pointed forward, to the left side of the boat. "Jolene, go on the starboard side." He pointed to the right. "Carolyn, get up at the bow." He waited until we were all in position.

"Listen. Very. Carefully. It's too dark for me to see much from back here. I need you to be my eyes and ears. Watch the water near you. If you see white water, even a tiny bit of foam, yell. If you hear rushing water, yell."

He was not about to quit again. He didn't want to face that sand bar another day. Despite the approaching darkness, we were going to keep trying.

I peered at the water. Mom's eyesight was not the best. Even with her thick glasses on, she had trouble seeing far away, especially in the dark. I studied the water around me, but I glanced periodically at the water in front of the bow, too, just to be sure. The water began to look black in the half-light. Looking this way and that, all around, I searched for foamy, white water that indicated something solid lurking below the surface.

"White water! Just ahead! Turn! Turn! Turn!" Mom shrieked.

Dad moved the tiller, trying to avoid the danger that he couldn't see.

"No, no! Not that way!" She waved frantically. "Turn the other way, the other way! Starboard!"

"Why didn't you say so in the first place?" Dad snapped as he corrected his turn. After a few moments, moments that seemed to last for hours, he wiped his forearm across his head. "Are we clear yet?"

The patch of white water passed by, just a couple of yards away. It wasn't big, but even a skinny rock could do serious damage to the hull.

"We're going to miss it," I yelled.

"Coast's clear," Mom yelled, at the same time.

It was too soon to breathe a sigh of relief, though.

I blinked to clear my vision and rubbed my eyes. Time seemed to move so slowly.

"Port, port! Turn port!" Mom screamed.

Dad yanked the wheel. The boat leaned and I grabbed the rail to steady myself.

I strained to see through the deepening darkness. I couldn't hear any rushing water, just the usual sounds of slapping ropes and gentle swishing water gliding past the hull.

After what seemed like hours, Dad called out, "We did it! We're over! We did it!" He danced a little celebratory jig. Despite the darkness, we had finally crossed over the sand bar and made it safely to the ocean side.

"Are we going to move out of the channel and anchor?" Mom asked with a yawn.

Just then, the moon came out, big and bright. Suddenly, we had light again.

"No. Now that we've got light, we should just keep going. Let's get back out to sea. Put some distance between us and that wretched sand bar." Dad steered by the light of the moon, and set a course toward the Cape of Good Hope.

All down the eastern coast of Africa, we'd fought storm after storm. The winds had been contrary. We fought for days to make the slightest headway. After crossing the sand bar, we were back in the same conditions. As soon as one gale died, another storm hit from a different direction. Sailing around Africa was desperate work.

Day after day, storm after storm hit. Walls of water hit, filled the bilge with water, and threatened to sink us. The compass light no longer worked. Its battery was damaged when the *Berenice* was thrown on its side. Dad's sextant was also broken, so he couldn't calculate our location any more. Dark bags hung under Dad's eyes. Mom drooped like a rag doll. They dragged themselves about. Around the clock, despite wide yawns, nodding heads, and utter exhaustion, they took turns at the helm and the bilge pump. With no crew, they had no relief, no time for even a brief break.

Eight days out of Inhambane, Dad called a family meeting in the galley. "I've done all I can, but these storms are too much. I need you to pray that these winds calm down, so we can get safely to Durban. Okay?"

Everyone nodded. Dad quietly said a prayer. I closed my eyes and said, "Please, make the storms go away and get us to Durban safely."

"Amen," everyone replied. Then Jolene and I went to bed. Dad and Mom left the main cabin, with baby Jackie, headed for the aft cabin.

While Mom could see through her coke-bottle-thick glasses during the day, at night she was practically blind. Yet, after Dad collapsed in utter exhaustion, she took over the helm. She couldn't bring herself to lie down, despite her fatigue. Dad advised her to dart between the waves, but they both knew that between her eyesight and the storm conditions, she was unlikely, even with a lantern, to manage to see the waves.

"Please, let them have a swift, easy death," Mom prayed as she stood alone at the wheel.

A large wave collapsed on the deck, drenching Mom. The cockpit flooded for a few minutes, but the water drained away, out to sea, as the yacht designer intended. Somehow, the Berenice shook it off and continued sailing.

Over the tumult, Mom heard Jackie scream in the aft cabin. Mom yelled at Dad, trying to get his attention, trying to get help for the baby, but he was dead to the world. Jackie's screams continued, but Mom couldn't let go of the wheel and attend to her. Bitterly cold and wet, despite her foul-weather gear, Mom clung to the wheel, listening to the baby scream, sure that the end was near, for hours.

Eventually, Dad awoke. Little Jackie was soaking wet and ice cold. The huge wave that hit earlier had splashed through the door slats and drenched her. Everything onboard was wet, so there were no dry blankets for warming the baby. Stripping off her wet clothing, Dad laid the ice-cold child across his stomach to warm her with his body heat.

Then Mom came down, stripped off her rain gear, and collapsed clutching the now sleeping baby, while Dad, reenergized from a few hours of sleep, took over at the helm once more.

In the morning, we woke up. Sometimes just waking is a miracle, an answer to prayer. The boat was steadier. The slight breeze was a welcome change from previous days, and we had made it through the night. Rain fell, but the wind dropped to a reasonable level. We'd almost forgotten that rain could fall without a heavy storm. Maybe our prayers had helped.

Dad thought we were close to Durban, though he couldn't be sure since the sextant was broken. He signaled passing ships, hoping to find out our location, but none noticed us. Mom and Dad were still exhausted, with barely enough strength to function. Worse yet, we ate the last of our food, and another storm brewed in the distance.

"Hello, aboard the ship!" came a booming voice. "Do you require a tow?"

On December fifteenth, South Africa's version of the Coast Guard appeared out of nowhere. What a wonderful surprise! Maybe our prayers had helped more than we realized.

Dad gratefully accepted the offer. As we were towed to Durban, Dad swore, "This is it. I've had enough. I'm giving up sailing forever. I can't take this anymore. I'm done. Enough is enough."

Almost seven months after setting out from Hervey Bay, Australia, our journey was done. We hadn't made it around the world as planned. Dad would sell the *Berenice* as soon as possible and use the money to fly us home. We'd get back to a less dangerous life and become landlubbers again. Or so he planned, but plans are subject to change . . .

25. Mozambique, Again

"Guess what?" Dad bounced from the wharf onto the boat. A deep dimple indented each cheek at the edges of his beard and a grin filled its center. "I've sold the *Berenice*! We'll buy airplane tickets back home and have enough money left to start over."

Mom raised an eyebrow and asked, "Who'd you sell her to?"

"Bloke named Jed. Met him at the Durban Yacht Club. He wanted to buy a boat for his company, his family's company really. Thought our yacht sounded perfect. He wants to see for himself that she's seaworthy. Besides, South Africa won't let us take that much money out of the country. Currency restrictions, you know. The plan is for us to sail back to Mozambique with him. Let him see how she handles, and we'll finish the deal there."

We were shocked. We weren't shocked that he was selling the boat, but that he planned to sail back through those storm-filled waters that had driven him to quit sailing. Yet if that were the only way to sell the boat and get enough money to continue, then we'd sail three hundred miles northward along Africa's east coast back to Mozambique. At least we'd end up with a nice amount of cash. Jed wanted the *Berenice* closer to the Suez Canal since his company was based in Israel, so it was the perfect solution for us all.

Mom shook her head slightly, shrugged her shoulders, and climbed down into the main cabin where seven-month-old Jackie waited for her supper of mashed banana.

Jolene and I moved our belongings out of the forward bedroom and back into the galley. Jed took over the private bedroom.

The return trip wasn't exactly smooth sailing, but it was much easier than the original voyage.

In Lourenco Marques, Mozambique, Dad and Jed set about the business of legally transferring ownership of the *Berenice*. Jed sent his copy of the contract to company headquarters in Israel, and we waited for the deal to be finalized.

Since Jed would soon own the boat, we moved into a hotel to wait for our money. Tiny by most standards, the rooms were spacious compared to those onboard. We swam in the saltwater swimming pool built on the edge of a cliff, where we could gaze at the ocean far below. There was even a maid to clean for us, which took some getting used to.

"Oh, no! My necklace!" Jolene yelped. Beads tinkled across the hotel floor, as Jolene scrambled to pick them up.

"Leave them for now. You'll have to pick them up when we get back," Mom insisted. "We're going to lunch. Come on, everybody else is ready."

Jolene pouted as she glanced back at the necklace she'd made herself. Dad held the door open, and we left the room, but on our return, the room looked different. The maid had cleaned up.

"Where are they?" Jolene looked around for her beads. They were gone.

Later, there was a knock at the door. A maid offered a string of polished brown berry beads to replace the cheap ones she'd picked off the floor.

"Oh, those are beautiful. They've got to be worth much more than yours," Mom told Jolene. Living in a hotel definitely had its perks.

Dad left the hotel the next morning to carry out some business. When he returned, something was wrong. His smile was gone. He was quiet, with his brows knit in thought. He and Mom conferred quietly in their bedroom, before scurrying to pack. A few minutes later, we checked out of the hotel and returned to the *Berenice*, which was moored upriver near a native village. Apparently, we would stay with Jed until the deal was finalized.

As soon as our belongings were aboard, Dad gave us a quick hug. "I'll be back in a few days, girls. You be good for your mother." Then he dashed off in a taxi.

"Where's Dad going?" I asked.

"To the airport to catch a flight to Israel," Mom said in a subdued tone. She rubbed her hip, and I heard the crinkling sound of paper.

Why did Mom have paper hidden under her clothes? Why was Dad taking a sudden trip? How did he get enough money to fly to Israel? Whatever was amiss, clearly no one was going to explain it to me.

Early the next morning, we caught a bus into town. The loud rickety vehicle, rusty with spots of faded paint, was crowded with chattering dark-skinned natives. The men wore plain pants and colorful shirts. The women covered their hair with brightly colored scarves, and wore several layers of skirts and blouses, with each layer a different color and pattern. Some carried cloth-wrapped bundles on their heads. A number held squawking chickens, small bleating goats, or other animals. Sweat, animal dung, and smoky fuel scented the air inside. Once the bus began moving, billows of dust from the bumpy, dirt road poured in through the open windows.

"Why did we have to leave so early?" I asked.

"These markets butcher their meat first thing in the morning and then let it hang out all day. Better to get there early, so the food's safer."

When we got off at the open-air market, Mom bought some fruits, vegetables, bread, and a bit of meat, but buying milk was a problem. Each dairy farmer shook his fists and scolded her with rapid-fire words of another language. Mom held her money out and used her tried and true signals to indicate what she wanted, but the milk sellers only grew more agitated.

"I don't understand what's wrong. The baby needs milk. Why won't they sell it to me?" Mom muttered to herself as she shook her head.

"Excuse me. I might be able to help." A smiling English-speaking woman, clearly a foreigner, spoke up. "You're trying to buy milk without a container. Their bottles aren't for sale. If you bring a jug, they'll fill it for you."

Milk would have to wait until we could return with a clean, used milk jug, but at least we now understood how to buy it.

Later, back on the yacht, Jolene and I entertained ourselves as usual. I read, played with blocks, or did my lessons—my second grade lessons were almost finished. Mostly, though, we kept quiet. Jed barked a lot, clearly upset that we'd invaded his space. Mom was jittery, startling easily, and always kept those papers hidden in her girdle.

One afternoon, Jed brought a strange man onboard.

"Here it is." Jed grabbed his rod from the storage hooks on the galley wall. The fishing pole hung directly over my head as I sat on a berth. "You'll like the action on this. It's smooth." He spun the reel before handing it to the newcomer.

Something flashed past my face. The cabin turned red and a metallic taste flooded my mouth.

A hook, now dripping red, dangled from the end of the fishing line in the stranger's hand. The two men stood, wide-eyed, staring at me. Time seemed to have stopped. No one moved.

Then I screamed. "Mom!" I sat still as a statue, afraid to move, afraid I might make it worse. Blood covered my face, though I wasn't sure where it came from.

Mom ran from her cabin.

"What's the mat . . . ?" She stopped suddenly. Her eyes took in the scene.

The men jerked, as though suddenly woken up. Everyone began moving.

"The hook is already out. You'll be fine," Mom said briskly, trying to keep me calm. "We just need to have someone take a look at you."

Grabbing me by the hand, she hustled to a cabstand. She went from cab to cab until she found a taxi driver who spoke English. After explaining the situation to him, he rushed us to the nearest village hospital, where he rattled off a lot of Portuguese to the hospital staff. A nurse whisked me away to a room where I was lifted onto a cold, metal table. The sterile alcohol smell of the hospital combined with the smell of my own blood. Mom remained in the waiting room. Strangers in white coats and masks surrounded me.

There were no beds in the room, just this table, the plain white walls, and a cabinet. I heard rustling sounds. Behind me, women did something.

A man in a white lab coat, stethoscope around his neck, marched into the room. He yelled orders. Metal instruments slammed onto a tray. He spoke to me in a soothing tone, but I didn't understand a single word.

A white cloth covered my face. If the cloth was supposed to keep me from seeing what they were about to do, it didn't work. Its large hole covered not only my torn upper lip, but my left eye, too. A needle came toward my face. I considered closing my eyes, but I couldn't do it. I tensed up. My eyes felt twice their usual size. I concentrated on not crying and waited for the pain. The needle moved so slowly. Then it hit. I felt a tug as it pulled through my upper lip, again and again. Three ugly pieces of black thread were knotted through my lip.

A nurse led me back to the front desk, where Mom waited. The woman in white spoke rapidly, with lots of hand movements, until Mom's repeatedly shrugged shoulders made it clear she understood none of it.

The nurse tried again. She spoke slower and used fewer words, but it didn't help. We had no idea what she was telling us. She signaled for us to wait, and then she left. We waited and waited. Finally, another woman in a white dress approached.

"Ten. Ten day," she said in halting English. She held up ten fingers.

"Ten days? Come back in ten days? Is that what you mean?" Mom made sure she'd understood correctly.

"Yes, ten days," the pretty nurse repeated, with a smile. She pointed at my lip and made motions as though she were pulling at the stitches.

I was to return in ten days to have the stitches removed, but that wouldn't be possible. Mom would remove the stitches herself, since we would have to escape soon.

26. Escape at Midnight

"Dad, you're back!" I yelled excitedly, as he strode down the dock.

"What happened to you, Pumpkin?" He pointed to the black threads on my face, before jumping over the rail onto the deck.

I explained the accident. He gave me a hug and then turned to Mom, who stepped into the cockpit, drying her hands on a dishtowel.

"Do you still have them?" He held his breath.

Mom reached into her girdle and pulled out some crumpled folded papers. "Yes, I was afraid he'd take them, so I kept them on me always."

Dad closed his eyes and exhaled. Then he nodded. "Good. With these ownership papers, Jed could have taken off with the *Berenice* and we'd be stuck," he said, grimly. "Our suspicions were correct. Jed fed us a pack of lies. Well, half-truths, anyway." Dad turned his head, first one way, and then the other. "Speaking of the devil, where is Jed?"

"He's gone." Mom shrugged, shaking her head. "This morning, he grabbed his belongings and left, without an explanation."

"Hmph! No surprise there. As I said, it was all a bunch of half-truths." Dad slammed a fist into the palm of his other hand. He paced up and down the deck. "His family, true enough, owns the company, but he's the black sheep of the family. They want little to do with him. The company does want to buy a boat, but not a yacht. They want a commercial fishing boat. They don't want a yacht and won't pay for one, and he knew it from the start. I think we foiled his plans by moving you girls back onboard so he couldn't sneak off with the boat."

"So there's no deal? No sale?" With a sigh, Mom plopped on a cockpit bench.

"No. No sale." After a brief silence, Dad added, "It isn't all bad news. An Israeli official heard about the *Berenice*. Saw pictures of it. He was impressed enough to offer me a job making ferro-cement boats for the Israeli government."

"And?" Mom asked.

"I told him I'm not interested, but he said if I ever change my mind, the offer stands. They'll fly us all out there."

"So what are we going to do now?" Mom asked quietly.

The sounds of lapping water and birds calling floated through the air, along with an occasional creaking sound from the rigging. The water around us sparkled from the bright sunlight.

Finally, Dad muttered, "I don't know. I just don't know. If only I had a sign from above telling me what to do." He looked up as though expecting a placard to drop from the clouds.

Later that afternoon, a stern-looking uniformed police officer visited the *Berenice*. "This needs to be paid," he demanded as he shoved a paper in Dad's face.

"What?" Dad reached for the document. A long list of figures ran down the page. "It's in Portuguese. What's the bill for?"

"Telephone bill. You must pay." The policeman sneered as he patted the gun in the holster at his waist.

"What does this have to do with us? We didn't make these calls." Dad handed the page back.

The policeman pulled out a small notebook and flipped through its pages. "These calls were made by a man named Jed. You know this Jed?"

"Yes, we know him, but he's gone. I don't know where he is. Doubt he'll be coming back." Dad explained Jed's attempted shady deal to the policeman.

"No matter. These were charged to the *Berenice*. This is the *Berenice*. You're the captain of the *Berenice*. So, you need to pay this bill." He pointed to the large multi-digit number at the bottom of the page. Apparently, Jed had made lots of long, expensive international calls.

"But why me? You know I didn't make the calls. Why don't you go after the man who did?" Dad asked.

"Because you are here. You are here," the man repeated, jabbing a finger at Dad with each word. "Pay this bill by tomorrow or I'll be back, and you'll go to jail."

After the officer left, Dad turned to Mom. "Well, Carolyn, I wanted a sign. I think I just got one."

"What do you mean? We haven't got that much money. What are we going to do?" Mom wrung her hands together.

"Didn't you hear? He said we'd have to pay because we're here. Because we are here. I think that's a pretty good sign that we aren't supposed to be here. We need to be somewhere else, so we're getting out of here tonight, before he comes back. We can't afford to pay someone else's bill, and we shouldn't have to," he said firmly. "It's bad enough that we sailed back all this way for nothing."

"But the harbor patrol . . . They won't let us out without clearance, and we won't get clearance if they think we owe money here," Mom pointed out.

"We can get out if they don't see us," he said, with a grim smile.

Dad had no time to repair the sails damaged on the trip to Mozambique. He couldn't afford to buy new ones even if there was time to order them. Instead, he found some sailors who were willing to help.

Sailors who cruise the world are a tight-knit lot. They become neighbors and friends, running into each other repeatedly as they cruise similar routes. They help each other, few questions asked, knowing that someday they may need assistance in return.

Dad soon returned with borrowed sails that he'd leave at the Durban Yacht Club for the owner to pick up eventually. Dad had promised to pass it along, to help someone else in need when he could. In fact, a few months later Dad kept this promise when he gave a sail to a Frenchman whose yacht was nearly destroyed by a storm. His mast broke in half, and his boat capsized. His girlfriend, trapped in the upside-down boat, drowned. The sailor eventually righted his boat and hobbled into Durban, but all his equipment was damaged or destroyed. He desperately needed help. What goes around comes around, so Dad gave him a sail, while other sailors gave what they could until he was re-outfitted. The Frenchman, an artist, painted pictures for them, as he wanted to repay their generosity somehow. That is the way of the sailing community.

Another man offered us help with his motorized dinghy. He'd tow the *Berenice* out of the harbor, helping us make a faster getaway. Dad didn't want to accept. He didn't want to include anyone else in the trouble that would come our way if we were caught. He didn't want someone else sent to jail, too, for something he hadn't done, but the man insisted on helping.

By late afternoon, we were ready. We ate supper early. Mom and Dad ate silently. Then we waited. We waited for the sun to go down, waited for darkness to fall, waited for the harbor to settle down for the night, and waited until all lights were off. We waited until midnight.

"No talking. Don't rattle anything. Be very, very quiet. We don't want to attract the harbor patrol's attention," Dad reminded us again in a low whisper. Then he carefully went up on deck.

I was wide-awake, despite the late hour. Normally, I would have been asleep at this time, which was long past my bedtime, but tonight I had a job to do—an important job. I had to make sure baby Jackie and Jolene didn't wake up and make noises. Not that anyone worried about Jolene waking, but seven-month-old Jackie might. I was armed with a bottle to quiet her, if necessary, since Mom and Dad would be busy on deck.

The night was dark, very dark. No lights were on, nor was the moon shining. The only noises came from creaking rigging of ships in the harbor, water sloshing around us, and the low sound of the dinghy's engine.

Cautiously, we made our way across the harbor. I stared through the porthole into the darkness. Listening intently, I strained to hear any unusual noises, noises that would indicate something wrong. We moved slowly for what seemed a very long time. Surely, we should be out of the harbor by now.

Suddenly, a bright light cut the darkness. I froze. The light moved around the harbor. It was a searchlight! The light on a harbor patrol boat turned this way and that. Slowly, it circled all around us and then came back toward us. Oh, no! They were looking for us! They must have heard us.

Our friend turned off the dinghy motor, but both boats continued to glide along, powered by inertia, heading toward the mouth of the harbor. The dinghy's pilot had his oars ready, if needed, to pull us onward, as silently as possible.

We were almost there. We were almost out of the harbor. Almost to the freedom of the sea.

I prayed silently, frantically. What would happen to us? Would we all end up in jail? Even us kids? I tried not to move, not wanting to do anything that would make noise or attract the harbor patrol's attention.

The search light paused.

"Halt! Stop!" an officer on the harbor patrol boat ordered through a megaphone. Through the porthole, in the dark shadows on the harbor patrol boat, I could make out something in his hands. Was it a gun? Were they going to shoot us?

The search light pointed right at another boat. The harbor patrol officers noisily boarded it, while we quietly sailed past and snuck right out of the harbor.

We waved a silent farewell to the good man who'd risked his freedom, maybe even his life, to tow us. Then Dad raised the sails. We headed out to sea. We'd made it! We were safe!

27. Surgery in the Women's Room

January 1972

Favorable winds pushed us to South Africa. No storms harried us this time. We reached Durban once again, this time without much trouble.

We hadn't sold the *Berenice* as planned. We needed money for food and supplies. Dad, who had been a surveyor in the United States Air Force, found work as a surveyor at the Louis Botha International Airport, and we settled into life in Durban.

As in Australia, a new school year began in South Africa in January, so I was now a third grader. However, in South Africa, they called it standard one instead of third grade. Jolene was in school now, too. She was in class A, or first grade. Together we walked several blocks each day to St. Joseph's Government School. Previously it had been a privately-run Catholic school, and its old name, St. Joseph's Girls' School, was still engraved over the entrance. I felt sorry for the boys who walked through that entrance each day.

Most of my lessons were in English, one of the South Africa's official languages, but I also learned Afrikaans, the other official language. Learning simple words and phrases was fun.

"Een, twee, drie, vier, vyf, ses, sewe, agt." I practiced counting at home on the boat.

"Ugh!" Jolene shuddered and held her hands to her ears. "Nasty."

"What's wrong?" I asked.

"That last word," she muttered.

"Agt?" I asked.

"Yes!" She grimaced. "Sounds like you're about to spit."

"But that's how you're supposed to say it." Naturally, I said the word a few more times to annoy her.

After learning at home for so long, school seemed strange. The lessons were easy enough, and being around other kids was interesting. Well, most of the time. Schools everywhere have bullies who terrorize others when the adults aren't looking. Mostly, I was amazed at how much time in school is spent sitting still, doing nothing but waiting. So much wasted time!

I wore a uniform to school. Well, two actually. The everyday uniform was a sickly-looking pale green short-sleeved cotton dress. The exercise uniform was the same horrid color but sleeveless and shorter.

Remaining from its days as a Catholic school, several nuns were on staff. The Catholic children attended mass regularly, while some of the rest of the students gathered in my teacher's room. She wasn't a nun. She read Bible stories aloud until the religious services ended.

My favorite time in school was Thursday afternoon. While the boys from my class attended woodworking class, we girls had sewing and knitting lessons downstairs with an elderly nun who strove for perfection.

"No good. Take them out. Do it again. Straighter," she ordered when I showed her my row of decorative stitches. This wasn't the first time I'd redone this row.

"Bah! No good. Make them smaller. Neater." She thrust my latest effort back at me.

Finally, after stitching the same row a twelfth time, she looked at my work and heaved a heavy sigh. She shook her head and growled, "All right. You may begin the next row."

She wasn't pleased with my work, but I thought the stitches looked fine. Great, in fact. I was proud of my work.

Walking home from school, Jolene and I often stopped to play along the way. A large grassy park, with a sunken entrance between tall green hedges, held a beautiful carved fountain that sprayed water high in the air. Colorful flowers and simple benches surrounded the fountain. The long lawn offered plenty of room to run and play. Mom didn't mind if we played there, since the boat was so cramped. It was nice to run in wide-open spaces for a change. Other children played in the park, too, often with a maid sitting on a bench nearby, reading a book as she watched over the children.

There we met Amerigo and his sister who lived in a nearby skyscraper and visited the park often.

With Mom's permission, we accepted their invitation to visit their home one afternoon for tea. From their windows, we saw the harbor far below. From that vantage point, the boats were too small to be sure which was the *Berenice*. Their apartment seemed spacious compared to our home. As tidy as a magazine picture, it seemed unimaginable that children actually lived and played here.

As we chatted, I discovered that Amerigo had never gone to school even though he was my age. He learned at home informally, but soon he would start boarding school far away in England. I couldn't understand how he could go to another country without his family, but he thought it was the usual educational plan.

Whack!

Amerigo and I jumped as a loud crash reverberated through the apartment. We ran, looking for our little sisters, to see what had happened.

Jolene stood by the kitchen door. Her strawberry blonde hair was cut pixie-style, a result of a recent experiment with scissors. Her face was ashen as she held out a hand and screamed. Tears streamed down her face.

"The wind shut the door. Shut it on her finger," Amerigo's sister explained over Jolene's howls.

"You'd better take her home," the maid added. She gave Jolene ice to hold on her thumb that had turned a nasty dark purple.

At home, Mom took one look at it and rushed us to the yacht club.

A doctor in white cotton knee-length shorts and a matching button-down shirt arrived a few minutes later, carrying a black leather bag. Mom explained what had happened, but when she asked Jolene to show the doctor her injury, Jolene refused, howling louder. After some coaxing, she finally showed the purplish-black thumb to him.

Soon the doctor cleared all non-employees out of the women's dressing room. He planned to use it as a makeshift operating room where he would remove her thumbnail. Some of the yacht club staff became temporary nurses. Lifting her on a table, he worked quickly, leaving her with a heavily bandaged thumb. He warned it would take months for a new nail to grow and ordered her to never rest her hand on a doorpost again—advice I doubt she needed.

28. WE'RE FAMOUS

One afternoon, Mom and we girls enjoyed afternoon tea at the Durban Yacht Club. The spacious dining room, with its cushioned chairs and wall-to-wall carpeting was a lovely change from the confined quarters of the *Berenice*. Sitting at a square table near a large window with a view of the harbor, Jolene and Mom sipped cups of coffee. Well, actually, Jolene had milk with a couple of drops of coffee in it, but she felt very grown up drinking her coffee. I couldn't stand the smell of coffee, so I drank a soda instead. Jackie sat in a stroller next to us, with a bottle of milk.

A man wearing cotton shorts and a light-colored shirt approached from a nearby table, with a newspaper in his hand. "Aren't you with the *Berenice*?"

"Yes, we are." Mom turned to face the stranger.

"I thought so. I saw your pictures in the paper when you first arrived in Durban. Did you see this article?" he asked, waving a folded newspaper.

"I don't think so," Mom said slowly.

"I thought you might like to read it since you're mentioned in it." He handed her the newspaper. "You can keep it," he added, with a smile.

We'd been in the news many times. Before our journey began, newsmen in both Australia and Missouri published stories about our intended voyage in newspapers or on television. Along the way, stories in various local newspapers relayed news of our trip. Nanny and Grandma regularly relayed news from our letters to the *Trenton Republican-Times* in Missouri so the whole town could follow our journey. This article was different, though.

I'd learned not to trust the media completely because every story about us included some incorrect information. It must be difficult to listen to someone else's story, understand the facts, and record them accurately. Yet, it was fun to read about ourselves.

This tiny back-page article told of a recent scientific expedition that began after scientists read a history of a tiny island in the Indian Ocean. Christian missionaries visited the island long ago and converted the natives. These missionaries believed alcohol was evil and convinced the natives to stop drinking their homemade beer. After a while, a plague of pain, paralysis, bloating, and such struck, leaving several dead. The islanders still clung to some of their old beliefs. Convinced that evil spirits had taken over the island, they climbed into their canoes and fled, leaving Egmont Island deserted. The scientists sailed to Egmont Island to learn more and ended their report with a note about a "curious bottle tree" on the island. Describing the very tree I'd found, the article included excerpts from a few of the posted messages, including ours about the *Berenice* and her inhabitants.

This explained why Egmont Island was deserted and yet full of fruit trees and paths into the jungle. A diet of only fish and fresh fruit, with too little thiamine, a B vitamin, left the natives suffering from beriberi and caused them to flee.

I'd been thrilled to explore the island's center. We'd hoped someone would someday find our note and read it, but I'd never dreamed my exploration would become part of a scientific paper reported in an African newspaper.

We were famous!

29. Girl Overboard

As time passed, we became used to life in Durban, though some aspects of South African life in the early 1970s were difficult to accept.

"You wouldn't believe what goes on at work," Dad ranted one evening in the privacy of our yacht. "The supervisor walked up to Damazeus, a Zulu warrior who works with us, and told him he looked like a monkey and worse. That man can't seem to treat any nonwhites decently. Did you know he only pays the black employees six cents an hour? Can you believe that? Six cents!"

"Why'd he call him names?" I asked.

"No reason at all that I could see. I apologized to Damazeus as soon as the guy was gone. Wish I could do something else to make it right. He's one of the hardest workers on the place." Dad sighed.

Yet, what goes around comes around. The bosses soon fired the nasty supervisor for poor surveying work, and they promoted Dad to take his place. Dad was eventually able to get the company to raise Damazeus' pay to ten cents an hour, but that didn't end the racial problems at work.

"What happened to you?" Mom asked one evening when Dad came home with several scrapes and bruises.

"You wouldn't believe it," Dad replied, slapping some papers against the galley table.

"Are you all right?"

"I'm fine." He spat the words out. "If we didn't need the money, I'd be out of that place like a light!"

"Sit down. Let me get you something to eat," Mom said, soothingly, as she set to work in the galley. "Why don't you tell me about it?"

"I was driving a company truck, a Ford Ranchero, down the road. A black man was wobbling on a bike at the side of the road. I didn't want to hit him, so I steered around him, but the road was wet. The truck hydroplaned and slid towards a concrete light pole. I wrenched the wheel around to avoid hitting it." He took a sip from the cup of tea Mom handed him.

"Oh, my!" Mom's hands stopped in midair. Her eyes widened as she stared at Dad.

"Don't worry. I missed the pole, but the truck flipped over two or three times. Tools were strewn along the road, and the truck was damaged some, but that wasn't the worst of it." Dad shook his head in disgust. "The bosses are mad that I didn't just hit the man. Said there'd be less damage to the truck if I had. I don't know how people like that can live with themselves. No respect for life."

Thankfully, we children experienced a different side of South African life.

"I win!" Jolene shrieked, laying her cards on the galley table as she bounced up and down happily.

"Beginner's luck," a tall, curly-haired young man cried from the other side of the table.

Another fellow in his late teens set down a bottle of soda on a tiny counter in the small cabin. A light breeze blew through the open hatch. Sunlight streamed through the portholes of this neighboring boat. "Poor sport," he teased. "Can't handle losing to a little girl." He laughed and punched his buddy on the arm.

"Thanks for teaching us to play rummy." I picked up the cards and neatly stacked them. Pointing at the tape recorder, I added, "Hearing ourselves on that machine was fun, too. We had a nice time. Thanks for inviting us over."

Climbing from their boat onto the wharf, Jolene and I stopped and waved at Hawsepipe who repaired a worn rope. A friendly old man, wiry, with leathery skin from years of working in the sun, Hawsepipe worked around the docks in Durban. He loved to chat and tell us stories. He kept an eye out for us, treating us like favorite nieces.

He waved back and leaned against one of the pier's supporting posts. Shaking the rope at us, he warned, "Don't you drink too much coffee." He must have heard about Jolene's drink at the yacht club.

"I started drinking coffee when I was a boy." He set the rope down, stretched his arms, and made himself more comfortable. "My mum told me not to, but I didn't listen. One day, I woke up to find my toes had turned black. The next day, my legs were black, up to my knees."

I didn't believe a word of it, but decided to play along. "Then why didn't you stop drinking coffee?"

He laughed. "Guess I didn't have any sense. I was too stubborn to listen. Just kept drinking coffee until I was black right up to my hair."

Jolene's eyes widened and her jaw dropped, but I protested. "People don't change color like that."

"Then how do you explain my black skin?" With a twinkle in his eyes and a lilt in his voice, he held out a dark arm.

I didn't know why some people have darker skin than others do, so I kept quiet.

At that time, South Africa divided people into three racial groups: white, black, and colored. According to the rules of apartheid, people of different races weren't allowed to live in the same towns, let alone go to the same schools. Multi-lingual signs around the country prohibited certain races from using specific beaches, businesses, and more. Worse yet, blacks were denied citizenship and weren't allowed to vote or travel freely within their own country.

But I hadn't noticed any of that. I didn't realize it was unusual for two fair-haired, pale-skinned little girls to befriend an ebony-colored man. I just knew he was a kindly old man, who entertained us with stories, and watched out for us.

A few days later, Jolene and I stopped at the Proctor and Gamble store after school. We loved riding their escalator, especially when the store wasn't busy, and we could run up the down escalator. Each of us held a half-cent coin. Until coming to South Africa, I'd never seen a coin worth half a penny. That little coin may not sound like much, but with it we could each buy a handful of candy. I picked out some licorice lollies, while Jolene bought some chocolates to eat on our walk home.

"Mom, we're home!" I yelled. After getting a drink of water, I asked, "Can we go play on the pier?"

"That's fine. Just stay close enough to hear me call when supper's ready." Mom let us wander around the harbor, playing on the pier or in the water, as long as we didn't roam too far. She wanted us to enjoy fresh air and exercise, and like most adults of that time, she thought children should have plenty of freedom.

The *Berenice* was tied to the end of a neat row of boats. To get to the pier, we had to climb over the *Berenice*'s rail, cross the deck of the neighboring yacht, then climb onto the next boat, and finally climb onto the yacht nearest the dock. From there, we could reach the pier's ladder.

The tide was extremely low, so the top of the pier towered above us. Tilting my head until it touched my back, I could see the top of the pier. Thankfully, the ladder was securely nailed to the dock.

I'd never liked ladders. Ever since I'd scaled one back in Australia, to take a tour of the *Berenice* before she was finished, nightmares of ladders plagued me. In them, the ladder would wait until I was near the top before it pushed away from its support. I was sure the nasty thing laughed as I screamed and plummeted earthward. As long as I didn't look down, I could climb this very tall one despite my fears.

This time, Jolene raced ahead, wanting to climb the ladder first. I'm not sure what happened next, but I heard sobbing.

"What happened?" I hurried to catch up, but she gave no answer other than more tears.

After that, everything seemed to happen in slow motion, but I couldn't do a thing to stop it. Jolene stepped over the boat's railing. Still crying, she grabbed the ladder's sides and stepped on a rung. Raising her other foot, tears must have clouded her view because she missed the rung and stepped into thin air. Nothing supported her as she lifted her lower foot. Screeching as she plunged like a lead sinker, she sank feet first into the murky water below.

I could see her, but I couldn't reach her. The surface of the water was much farther away than my arm could reach. Even an adult's arm couldn't reach her from the deck of this boat, and the pier was a good twenty feet higher.

I didn't know what to do. Jolene panicked, bobbing in and out of the water. She would drown if someone didn't grab her soon. She couldn't get enough air to scream. The *Berenice* was too far away. By the time I ran there for help, she'd be gone.

A thin, sandy-haired man stood on the dock above, gazing out at the harbor. He must not have seen the accident.

"Hey, mister!" I yelled. Startled, he looked down at me. "My sister fell in the water! Help!" I pointed at her as she thrashed wildly about, arms flailing.

To my surprise, the man just stood there. Frozen.

"There's a little girl in the water, mister. She needs help! Fast!" I screamed again.

He stood still as a statue. He did absolutely nothing. What was wrong with him? Why didn't he do something? Weren't grownups supposed to take care of things? Weren't they supposed to help children? What was his problem?

What could I do about it? I couldn't reach her myself. If I jumped in, I wouldn't be able to hold her. She was too wild for that. I looked around trying to think of a plan.

Pounding footsteps echoed from the pier above. I looked up and saw a flash as someone slid down the ladder and splashed into the filthy water below.

The frozen man on the pier suddenly jerked as though slapped. Then he jumped up and down, waving his arms, as he screamed, "Help! Help! Somebody help! A little girl's drowning!"

But the hero had already reached out a dark hand and grabbed Jolene under one arm. Plucking her dripping wet body from the water, he climbed a few steps and plunked her on the deck beside me. Jolene sputtered, coughing out water. She was soaking wet, but she was safe and sound. No thanks to the coward on the wharf.

Back on the *Berenice*, Mom hugged Jolene tightly and gave her dry clothes, while I explained what happened.

"Make sure you look where you're going at all times, young lady," Mom sternly warned her. "I don't want any of you children falling in again," she muttered.

Little did she know that Jolene wouldn't be the only one to fall over.

30. Little One Overboard

"What on earth?" asked Mom, when Dad came home from work one evening. In his arms, he held a long, brown dachshund. "A dog? Why on earth would you bring a dog on the boat?" she asked in surprise. They'd never discussed adopting a dog. Our pets in Australia were cats, so a dog was a huge surprise.

Dad set the dog on the deck, and Mom crouched down to pet the short dog with long, floppy ears. Jackie sat in the cockpit, where Mom had put her. She laughed, pointed, and made silly noises at the dog, while I stood and observed from the companionway. The dog lowered his head and sniffed here and there. Waddling about, he explored the deck. So far, he looked harmless enough.

"One of the men at work saw this poor little guy on a mountainside road. He wanted to run over him, rather than swerve around him. He said it was 'just a dog,' as though dogs aren't worth anything. I can't abide the attitudes some of the men here have!" he said in disgust. "I made him rescue the dog. The dog wasn't bothering anyone. Wasn't causing any trouble. There was no reason to harm him. One of the men took him to the pound, but they were going to destroy him. So, here he is."

"A dog? On the boat?" Mom looked around the deck. "How are we going to keep a dog? We don't have room for him. Dogs need space to run." Despite her words, the tone and tender look said she wouldn't send him back to the pound.

"The kids will take him on the pier for walks. He'll get used to life onboard. You'll see. Besides, he'll be good for Cheryl."

When I was a toddler, an over-enthusiastic dog had jumped on me. Pawing and nipping, the dog wasn't mean. Rather, no one had trained him to behave properly. However, I was little and the roughhousing frightened me. I'd been scared of dogs ever since. Dad hoped I'd grow to love him and overcome my fear.

"Hmm, you may be right." Mom looked from the dog to me and back again.

Jolene ran to the dog and stroked his fur. She wasn't afraid of any animal. "What's his name? Are we really going to keep him? I've always wanted a dog."

"Well, I thought we'd call him Harvey." Dad leaned against the mast and winked.

"Harvey? Like the invisible, white rabbit that steers for us sometimes?" she asked. "Then we'll have two Harveys."

"I think we'll be able to keep the two straight," Dad said with a chuckle. He moved near the dog, bent down, and scratched Harvey's stomach. Harvey made a funny gurgling sound in the back of his throat and rolled his eyes up at Dad. Clearly, he enjoyed the attention.

I kept my distance, watching Harvey carefully. He didn't bite or scratch anyone. He didn't do anything startling, but he took his time moving about. When the others left, he waddled around, sniffing everything, exploring his new home. He roamed from the stern to the bow. He didn't seem dangerous so far.

After school the next day, Mom handed me a leash. Harvey wore a collar, and she demonstrated how to attach the leash to it. "I want you to take Harvey for a walk. There's little room here for running around, even for a small fellow like him. He'll need exercise every day."

I looked at Harvey and his stubby legs. Then I glanced at the path to the top of the pier. There were boats to cross, rails to jump over, and the ladder to scale. His belly almost hit the deck as he waddled around on his short legs. He looked incapable of climbing anything.

"How's he supposed to get up to the dock?" I asked, dubiously.

"He isn't. You'll carry him, of course," Mom replied with an air of surprise. "Go on now. I have other things to do." She hesitated at the doorway and added, "And make sure he gets a nice, long walk. A very long one. He should be tired when you come back."

"Umm," I grunted at Harvey. "Come on. We're supposed to climb to the dock," I muttered, irritated at having another chore. I didn't want a dog. I hadn't asked for him, and I certainly didn't want to carry one up the ladder and give him a long walk every day. In fact, I didn't really even want to touch him.

I circled around him a couple of times, trying to decide the best way to pick him up.

"Hey, do you get to walk Harvey?" Jolene asked excitedly, bounding up from the cabin licking the remnants of her afternoon snack off her fingers. "I wish I got to walk him. You're lucky."

"Lucky? Well, you're not the only one who wishes you could walk him," I muttered.

I decided to put my forearms under his belly to lift and carry him. Gingerly, I stepped forward, cautiously approaching him. He didn't bark or snap. He just looked at me with big dark eyes, as if he wondered what I was doing and why I was taking so long.

"Okay," I said to myself. I bent down. "He won't hurt me. I can do this."

Eventually, I picked him up. "Oof!" I said, as my legs threatened to collapse under me. "You're a lot heavier than I expected. Maybe you need to go on a diet."

Harvey said nothing. The smell of damp dog filled my nose, making me sneeze several times.

"Unh!" Grunting, I managed to put one leg over the railing and bounced a couple of times, shifting my feet into a better position, before I lifted the other foot over. Going up the ladder would be more challenging. Staring at it, I tried to imagine how I could hold this heavy little fellow while also holding the ladder. Maybe I should scoot my arms farther apart under his belly. I set him down for a moment and shifted my arms. Could I grab both sides of the ladder while holding him?

"Grrugga." Harvey made a grumbling sound, as if he asked what on earth I was doing to him.

Slowly, deliberately, I stepped off the boat and onto the ladder. Concentrating, I carefully made my way up. Thankfully, the tide wasn't low, so the climb was only a few feet. Finally, I placed Harvey on the dock, and he turned to look at me. His tongue bobbed up and down as he waited patiently for me. Once I was on the dock too, Harvey bounced a little. He was anxious to go.

We walked down the pier and onto the shore. We roamed up and down the ramps that were used to lower boats into the water. We explored other docks and meandered around the Durban Yacht Club's parking lot. When we finally returned, Harvey panted heavily and seemed ready for a rest.

Carrying him back down to the boat was no easy task, but I managed it, while telling Harvey that the walk might help him lose some weight.

We'd been on the *Berenice* for more than a year now. Jackie never learned to crawl since there wasn't enough space for it on the boat. However, she had learned to pull herself up, holding onto the berths to support herself, and had even taken a few steps while holding on.

"Ahoy the ship! Give us a hand?" someone yelled. Another boat wanted to tie up alongside the boat next to us, at the end of the row of boats. Jolene, Mom, Dad, and I all ran to the deck to help as much as possible while also meeting our new neighbors. The sun shone brightly. A light breeze caressed my skin.

We jumped onto the boat next to us and joined its owners on their deck. The new vessel maneuvered slowly, as it came close enough to tie up. Old tires, each tied to a line, were thrown over the side to act as cushions, to keep the boats from damaging each other when they bumped. We all stood, leaning over the side, grabbing for the new boat's rails to guide it safely into position.

Dad grabbed a line a sailor tossed and secured it to the stern. A neighbor grabbed another line and tied the two boats together at the bow.

"Welcome aboard!"

"Nice to meet you!"

"Where are you folks from?"

"Where are you headed?"

"Are you planning to stay long?"

Greetings and questions flew back and forth.

Splash!

We all stopped. Something sizeable had fallen into the water. What was it? What made that sound?

We looked around. Harvey padded about on our deck, looking mournfully at us on the next boat over. He hadn't fallen in. All the equipment was there. Nothing seemed to be missing. What could it be?

"Ugh!" Mom screamed suddenly. Her face lost all color. Her eyes doubled in size.

At almost the same instant, Dad cried in agony, "Oh!" He leaped over the cabin and flew across the deck. He stopped and bent over. Anxiously he scanned the water, searching for a sign, anything, something to show where to look.

Mom sprinted across the boat almost as fast as Dad did. The rest of us weren't far behind.

We stopped and stared into the dark, murky water, looking this way and that. Unlike the crystal clear waters we'd encountered on Australia's Great Barrier Reef, the water in Durban's harbor always seemed to have a greasy colorful sheen of oil on its surface. The water below was usually so muddy and murky it was impossible to see even a foot or two below the surface. When Jolene and I splashed and played in the water close to shore, we encountered lots of garbage and filth.

No ripples marked the surface. Nothing floated. What made that noise? Where did it happen?

"There!" Dad screamed. "The white spot!" He dove in.

About halfway down the sloping hull of the *Berenice*, submerged under a couple of feet of water, was a small patch of white. It didn't look like a fish or anything else normally in this murky water. It floated just below the surface of the water.

Dad swam directly to it. A moment later, he popped out of the water, gasping for air. He raised his hands, lifting the white diapered bottom of Jackie. A neighbor leaned over the railing, stretching his arms to grab the baby. Dad lifted her, tried to hand her to the fellow, but he couldn't hold her high enough. He tried again, but he couldn't do it.

Splash!

Mom jumped in. She grabbed Jackie and with a burst of unbelievable strength, bounced high enough out of the water to hand the baby to the neighbor who laid her down.

We crowded around Jackie, worried, wanting to help. Mom and Dad climbed back on the boat. Dripping wet, they pushed their way through the crowd to reach the toddler.

Jackie coughed and sputtered. A neighbor turned her over and pumped his hands against her stomach. She vomited and coughed a few more times. Then she looked around, confused, as if trying to figure out what everyone was looking at.

Dad stood hunched over. He slowly shook his head as he stared at Jackie. Mom trembled violently from head to toe. She burst into tears, something I'd never seen before.

"Get some towels and blankets," Dad ordered. "She's going into shock." I wasn't sure if he meant Mom who sobbed uncontrollably, or the baby who wasn't happy either. Maybe he meant both of them.

Clearly, Jackie had followed us when we ran to the next boat. Though she'd never done it before, she climbed the short ladder to the deck and toddled to the railing. She must have tried to cross from the *Berenice* to the neighboring boat.

We were very thankful that Dad had spotted her white diaper under the hull of the *Berenice*. Never again would we leave Jackie alone. Not even for a minute.

31. THE BEST CREW EVER

By early 1973, Dad had earned enough money to restock our supplies and had repaired all the storm damage. The Louis Botha Airport didn't need surveyors anymore, so Dad was out of a job. The nine months spent in Durban's calm harbor lessened the horrific memories of the vicious storms, and hence we resumed our journey.

Mom bought fourth-grade curriculum from the Australian government for me. Jolene inherited my old second-grade materials, and we were homeschooled again.

David, a young man with curly light-brown hair and an infectious smile, wanted to travel with us as far as Cape Town, where his parents lived.

"Here, Cheryl." Dad handed me a small pill and a cup of water. "Swallow this."

"What is it?" I eyed the pill suspiciously. It didn't look like a quinine tablet. I wasn't sick. Why did I need medicine?

"It's Dramamine—a miracle medicine that prevents seasickness."

I dreaded the first three days at sea. I knew I'd be miserable, clutching my churning stomach, wanting to vomit, feeling dizzy. I'd stay sick until I earned my sea legs again. A pill that could cure that would be wonderful!

For three days, I took the pills and never felt sick. After three days, I earned my sea legs again and felt fine. It was a miracle!

However, our crew didn't fare as well. Oh, David didn't seem the least bit seasick, but Harvey was another story. Poor Harvey. His head hung low. He wouldn't eat. He lost weight. Pitiful moaning sounds came from deep in his throat. Dramamine worked wonders for me, but it was people medicine and wasn't meant for dogs.

With a heavy sigh, Dad announced, "I've found someone on shore who's willing to care for Harvey and give him a home. It's for the best, girls." The words didn't match Dad's sorrowful expression. His drooping mouth and hanging head mirrored poor Harvey. "We can't let Harvey stay so miserable. Clearly, he wasn't meant to be a sailor dog. We'll have to do what's best for him."

Tears welled up in Jolene's eyes. "I'll miss you!" she cried, wrapping her arms around his neck in a big hug.

Jackie patted Harvey gently. She didn't understand what was going on, but she knew we were upset and Harvey needed comforting.

I still didn't like dogs—at least, not other dogs—but I'd grown fond of Harvey, even though I still found walking him annoying. I waved sadly, as Dad put him in our new dinghy, and rowed him ashore. We would miss our furry little crewman.

David tried to distract us. He picked up a square I'd knit as a school assignment in Durban. "Did you make this by yourself?" He looked at it intently.

"Yes," I muttered, as I wondered if Harvey would miss me carrying him up the ladder.

"Well, I think I know something you'll like. It'll take me a while, but I'll have a surprise ready for you soon," he promised.

Later, he sat on the deck, holding a branch and a knife. He ran the knife along the wood, and peeled off a thin strip, which he let fall onto the deck. Again and again, he trimmed the wood. Slowly, he shaped it. Whittling, he called it.

A couple of days later, he triumphantly handed me a long, thin, round stick. Its pointed end stuck out a bit to one side. There was a neck just below it.

"I sanded it silky smooth." David looked at me expectantly.

"Um, it's very nice. What is it?" I finally asked, since I had no clue.

"It's a crochet hook." He waved it with a flourish.

"What kind of a hook?" I asked.

"A crochet hook," he repeated. Cocking his head, he gave me a puzzled look. "Don't you know how to crochet? I assumed you would, since you knit."

"No, I've never heard of crochet before. What is it?"

"Well, if you have some yarn, I'll show you," he offered.

With my yarn, he tied a slipknot and stuck the hook through the loop. Pulling the stick in and out, twisting the yarn around it somehow, he made a chain. He turned it around, pulled the hook in and out a few more times, and some fabric emerged. When he finished a square, he tied a piece of yarn to one corner and then another.

Lifting it proudly, he said, "It's an apron for your doll."

I had no idea how he'd done it, so I never used his crochet hook, but that creation proved he was different from our previous crews. There was other proof, too. He didn't ignore us kids but talked to us like real people. After supper, he taught us to sing folk songs such as "Kumbaya" and "Michael, Row the Boat Ashore" while we sat together in the cockpit, watching the sunset. Each Sunday afternoon, he brought out a bar of chocolate, and distributed a piece to everyone. Except for the M&Ms, we never had candy at sea, so this was a big treat.

He shrugged off our thanks. "Out here, far from everyone else, days are hard to tell apart," he explained. "I thought we needed a way to keep track of each new week." So every week, he brought out another chocolate bar. I liked David's calendar.

Along the coast, on our way to Cape Town, we stopped at a tiny port to stock up on freshwater, but the harbor and the nearby village had no running water. We carried empty buckets down a dirt path past the skeletal remnants of bushes to a small gathering of round grass huts. At the village well, we filled the buckets about three-fourths full. My arms felt stretched out of shape by the weighty burden. Hunched over, a bucket dangling from my hands, I trudged slowly back to the boat, trying to keep water from splashing out. My arms ached. The bucket handle dug into my palms leaving painful red indentations. Resting on the dock long enough for an adult to add the precious liquid to our tanks, I turned back down the dirt path to repeat the trek.

The ebony-skinned girls and women of the village wore brightly colored fabric around their hair and beautiful long cotton dresses with bright geometric designs. Some had a long strip of cloth tied over one shoulder with a baby held securely inside. They drew water from the well for their families, too, but they didn't struggle. Instead, they placed heavy earthenware jugs of water on their heads. They walked regally, at a steady pace, never using their hands to steady the jugs, so their hands were free to carry other things. Their way looked easy and graceful.

Back on the boat, I tried to imitate them. I put a book on my head and tried to walk across the galley without it falling off. It was much harder than it looked. After many attempts, I walked a few steps before the book fell to the floor. Of course, the motion of the waves, small as they were in the harbor, probably made the task harder.

After filling up, we continued around the tip of Africa, bound for Cape Town.

"What are those towers?" I asked one afternoon, as I stood on deck, gazing at the coastline visible in the distance. "I can see them though we're so far away. They must be huge." The grayish towers resembled branchless, leafless trees standing on the distant rocky coastline. Broad at the base, the structures narrowed at the top.

David sat on the aft cabin steering. Looking in the direction I pointed, he smiled and said, "Termite mounds. They're taller than most houses. Amazing creatures, really."

"What are?"

"Termites. They're an insect, like ants, but they fly and eat wood," he explained.

I didn't care for bugs. Insects that could build skyscrapers were definitely bugs to avoid, I decided, glad there was no nearby harbor and so we'd soon pass by those pests.

A few days later, the *Berenice* clipped along at a steady pace. A beautiful, steady breeze blew. The coastline had vanished in the distance, when a sail appeared on the horizon. We rarely saw other vessels this far out at sea, and when we did, they usually stayed far away. However, this yacht changed direction and headed toward us. As she drew near, several men waved and cheered from her deck.

"They seem friendly," Dad said, from his seat at the tiller.

Their captain yelled something. The sound of the waves slapping the hull combined with the stiff breeze drowned the words before they reached us.

Dad cupped his hands around his mouth and yelled back, "Ahoy there. Say again."

Eventually, they drew close enough for us to understand. "Ahoy! We haven't seen anyone else in a coon's age." Before cell or satellite phones or the internet, sailors were isolated at sea.

"Where you from?" he hollered. He and Dad compared notes on where they'd been, the weather along the way, and their destinations.

I'm not sure how it started. The other ship had bottles of beer. Mom had just made a cake, and soon a trade was arranged. Given the speed we were sailing, a trade wasn't easy. They couldn't throw the bottles of beer at us without breaking them on our deck, or sinking them to the bottom of the ocean if their aim was off. The cake wasn't likely to survive being tossed either, so another plan was formed.

The other yacht veered away, then came about, and headed toward us again. Mom climbed onto our bowsprit in the front of the *Berenice,* and with one arm, she held tightly to a cable supporting the forward mast. David handed her a wrapped chunk of cake. She leaned out over the water, while Dad maneuvered the *Berenice* into position. A sailor stood on the other ship's bowsprit, a sack of beer dangling from his free hand.

The boats plowed toward one another. A head-on collision seemed imminent, but at the last moment, Dad and the other helmsman pulled their respective wheels, and the boats sailed past each other. However, Mom still held her cake, and the sailor still held his sack.

Both boats circled around for another try. Mom straddled the railing, and inched farther out on the bowsprit. The fellow with the sack scooted further out on his bowsprit. Each adjusted their grasp of their respective packages. We were ready to try again.

Again, the two vessels aimed at each other, like two knights preparing for a joust. Through the waves, they plunged toward one another. Collision seemed certain. A last-minute tug on each wheel pulled them slightly apart and they plowed past each other, but this time, Mom clutched the sack, while the sailor held the cake.

Cheers and applause erupted. "Hurrah!"

"Yeah!"

Someone let out a long whistle.

"Great googa moogas!" Dad raised his fist triumphantly.

Mom climbed off the bowsprit and brought the sack over. Jolene and I huddled around her, watching as she opened it and pulled out the bottles of beer. Dad and David each grabbed a bottle and saluted the visitors with them. The men on the other ship waved pieces of cake in the air. Then they sailed off, heading toward Durban while we resumed our course to Cape Town.

"What's that in the bottom of the bag?" I asked.

Mom pulled out a piece of paper. Turning it over, she broke into a smile. "Oh! How lovely. Take a look." Mom held out a photograph. Of us! In it, the *Berenice* plunged through the Atlantic, with Dad at the tiller. David sat on the stern railing. Mom was in the cockpit, and my blonde head peeked out of the main cabin.

"How'd they do that?" I asked.

"It's a Polaroid photo. The camera spits out the photo instantly," Mom explained, handing it to Dad. "They must have taken it while sailing alongside. How thoughtful."

After Dad admired the picture, he pried the lid from his beer and took a swig. He and David toasted the yacht now disappearing from view.

Mom's voice grew wistful. "I think I'll put this away. It's a shame we don't have more photos."

The damp sea air had destroyed most of our photos, especially the color ones. Their surfaces dissolved, causing some to meld together, while only blotches of the original image remained on others. The photograph of us with the giant tuna was gone. Most of the family pictures from Australia were no longer. Thankfully, this photo would survive.

David would leave us at Cape Town. That was the plan from the beginning, but his farewell was unlike that of our other crewmembers. He didn't disappear after a quick good-bye.

"Want a tour of Cape Town?" he asked Jolene and me.

"Yes, please!" yelled Jolene.

"May we, please? Please?" I asked Mom, looking up at her with large pleading eyes and clasped hands.

"Well, we have to get ready for the long voyage across the Atlantic," Mom said slowly.

We expected to be at sea longer than ever before, so there was a lot to do to prepare. In the end, Mom let us go, saying that she could work faster without us under foot.

David took us to a local zoo, where we saw zebras, springbok, eland, ostriches, and other African animals. My favorite was the one-hundred-year-old tortoise. The zoo allowed children to climb on his back for a brief, plodding ride.

Then we took a cable car up to the summit of Table Top Mountain. The view through the windows was magnificent, though frighteningly high. As we rose through the air toward the mountaintop, the car swayed slightly, and I looked in vain for something to cling to for support. From the *Berenice*, the mountain looked flat on top, like a table, but stepping out of the cable car, I was surprised to see a very jagged and rocky surface that wasn't at all flat. At a little shack, David bought us each a long stick of hard candy with a design through the center. Mine looked like a flower in the middle, while Jolene's was a star. We sat on a boulder and licked the candy, while gazing at Cape Town far below.

The city's huge skyscrapers seemed to be toothpicks from this vantage point. David pointed out various places. He told us about famous landmarks, as well as where his family lived and he'd gone to school.

Afterwards, he took us to visit his mother. Wearing a lovely, light-colored frock, she had prepared a tea party in our honor in her garden. A small round table held beautiful china, buttered scones, and tiny squares of cake. Pulling a cover off a teapot, she poured tea for each of us and spoke to Jolene and me as though we were fine ladies. She proudly explained that she'd taught David to crochet when he was a boy, and asked questions about our journey thus far. It was a delightful grown-up tea party such as I'd read about in stories.

We were sad to say our final farewells to David. He'd been so wonderful. No one could replace him, and Dad didn't even try. From here on, we would have no crew.

32. Becalmed

On the eastern side of Africa, in the Indian Ocean, we'd fought storm after storm. Here on the western side, the weather was more favorable. We sailed along at a nice pace, enjoying ourselves, and with little of interest to report until April 25, 1973, when we stopped briefly at St. Helena, Napoleon's final home. Almost two weeks later, on May 8, we anchored for a few days at Ascension Island. The seas had been calm and the winds light in the Atlantic, but now they were too light.

Sailors nicknamed this equatorial region "the doldrums" for good reason. Sometimes the wind stopped completely. With no breeze nor an engine, the *Berenice* couldn't move unless a current—a river in the ocean—pulled her along. We had plenty of food and water. We weren't in a hurry. We had no better place to be, and being miserable about the situation wouldn't help, so we enjoyed ourselves instead.

"Let's go swimming!" Dad whooped. He pulled off his shirt and ran across the deck. He dove over the side. Water flew as he hit the ocean. "Come on in! The water's great!" he yelled, waving at us.

"Arrrh!" Jackie screamed.

"It's all right. Daddy's not hurt. See? He's having fun." Mom held her close and spoke in soothing tones, but Jackie was leery of water since her accident.

Jolene and I had no such fears.

"Can we, Mom? Can we go swimming? Please!" I pleaded, jumping up and down.

"Please, Mom?" Jolene echoed, as she wiped perspiration from her forehead. Her singlet, or t-shirt, was damp with sweat. Without a breeze, surrounded by solar-heated water, the air felt like a steam bath.

"Okay, girls. Get your bathing togs on." Mom held a hand to her stomach and plopped onto the cabin.

We raced to cabin door, but then I stopped, turned, and asked, "Don't you want to swim, too, Mom?"

"No thanks, dear. I'm not feeling so well. I'll just sit and be the lookout." Her face was pale and her eyelids drooped. "Besides, someone has to stay with Jackie."

"Are you okay, Mom? What's wrong?" I walked back over to her.

My mom never sat idle. Never. "Idle hands are the devil's workshop" had been drilled into her as a foster child, but today, she just sat.

"I'll be okay," she assured me. "I just feel a bit seasick." She reached over and patted my hand, but a minute later, she popped up and vomited over the side of the *Berenice*.

Something was definitely wrong. Mom had never been seasick before—not even during the cyclone. I watched quietly for a minute and then resumed my trip below deck.

When I came back, dressed in a bathing suit, Jolene was already in the water, splashing with Dad. Mom had put Jackie in the cockpit, where she couldn't see anyone in the water, and there the toddler played with a piece of rope. Mom watched everyone from her perch on the cabin. I sat at the edge of the deck. Then, I slid beneath the railing and into the cool, still water, and paddled over to Jolene and Dad. We bobbed around, splashing, and playing games in the water.

"Time for me to fix supper. Come on out," Mom called, an hour or so later.

"But, Mom . . ." I complained.

"Just a little longer," wheedled Jolene.

"No," Mom said firmly. "No lookout means no swimming."

We climbed onboard. The bright sun soon dried us. I grabbed a book and read stories to Jolene and Jackie, until time for supper.

Mom seemed fine now. Maybe nothing was wrong after all. Yet, the next day, Mom was sick again.

"Let's do something exciting," Dad suggested when the steamy blanket of afternoon air felt ready to smother us. "Watch this!" he hollered with a big grin and a sparkle in his eyes. He loosened one end of a rope lashed to the mast. Grasping the loose end, he leaped onto the cabin. Then he ran, letting out a wild yodel as he vaulted off the cabin top. Holding onto the rope, he swung far out over the sea. With another wild yell, he let go and plummeted into the ocean below.

Wow! That was crazy.

He quickly swam around to the stern of the *Berenice* and climbed up to the deck. Running to the cabin top, he grabbed the rope, took a running leap, flew into the air, and splashed down into the water, again.

"That looks like fun!" I said, clapping at his antics.

"We should try it," Jolene suggested, with a big grin.

I stopped giggling and looked at her. Me? Try that? I thought about it. How could I be sure that I'd jump far enough to land in the water? Maybe I'd smash into the deck instead.

"Um, I don't think so," I finally said. "I'll just watch." I sat on a cockpit bench, out of Dad's path, and watched. Jolene gazed longingly at the rope, but then she turned, and came and sat next to me.

"Shark! Shark! Wally, get out of the water!" Mom screamed. She pointed across the water where a shark's fin cut the surface. His shadowy body meandered under the water toward us. The splashing must have attracted his attention.

Dad scrambled out of the water and studied the shark as it glided to where Dad had been moments earlier.

"Well, no more swimming today," Dad said calmly. "Thanks, honey." He gave her a peck on the cheek, and then dried himself with the towel she offered. Minutes later, he stretched out on the deck with a cup of water and a book. Generally, he had lots of work, but becalmed for days on end meant little work was generated. There were no sails to mend, no repairs needed, and no messes to clean up.

Mom stood, with a hand on her stomach again. "Well, I've figured it out," she announced. "I haven't been seasick."

Jolene and I looked at each other. If she hadn't been seasick, then what was wrong?

"I've had morning sickness." Her smile matched Dad's grin. Dad hopped up and gave her a kiss on the cheek.

I looked over at Jolene and shrugged my shoulders. She shook her head at me.

"I'm expecting a baby," Mom explained. "In a few months, if all goes well, you'll have a little brother or sister."

I was relieved. Mom was fine. A new family member was something to look forward to, too.

33. VISITORS

Ptt ptt ptt ptt ptt. What was that noise overhead? It grew louder and louder.

We sat in the galley eating a quiet lunch. Putting down our utensils, we stared at the ceiling, listening intently to the increasing noise. Then Dad jumped off the berth and hustled up the ladder into the cockpit. The rest of us raced after him.

A helicopter approached, flying directly toward us. Rapidly dropping, it came nearer and nearer. Two men sat inside. The pilot wore a helmet and jumpsuit. A man in the back crouched near an open doorway, peering in our direction through binoculars. What were they doing out here in the middle of the ocean, far from anywhere?

The pilot turned his head and looked right at us. The other man leaned out, waved, and made some strange gestures. Water flew out of the sea as the spinning rotors aimed a stiff wind at the ocean below it.

"What does he want?" I yelled over the roar of the machine.

"Beats me." Dad shrugged.

The helicopter hovered overhead for a minute. Then it slowly circled us. After flying around us a second time, it turned and went back in the direction it came from.

"Huh? Wonder what that was about?" Dad stood watching, one hand at his forehead blocking the strong sunlight, as the helicopter disappeared over the horizon.

Little Jackie bounced like a rubber ball and pointed in the air. "What that?" she asked.

"A helicopter," Mom answered. "Okay, the excitement's over. Let's go finish our lunch." She led the way to the cabin door.

Faintly, I heard the puttering noise again.

"I think it's coming back!" I pointed at a black dot far off in the sky.

Louder and louder it grew. Then it dropped and hovered a few yards above the ocean, about a boat's length from us. The spinning rotors sent water spewing. I grabbed the side of the cockpit to steady myself against the stiff breeze it created.

The man in back leaned out of the open doorway again, but this time, he flung something into the water.

"Why'd he do that?" Jolene yelled.

"What is it?" I added.

A neon object bobbed up and down in the water a few feet away.

"I don't know, but clearly, they want us to get it," Dad replied as he grabbed a long, hooked pole. With the gaff, he reached over the side for the floating object. The helicopter still hovered, though higher in the air and further away now. Dad snagged the container and pulled it onboard.

Unscrewing its top, he reached in and pulled out a sheet of paper. "It's a note," he hollered over the roar of the helicopter, which had dropped again.

"What does it say?" Mom asked, as Dad unfolded the paper. Large crayon marks filled the page.

"If you are the *Boomer*, stand on the bow with arms up. If you are not the *Boomer*, stand on the bow with arms at your side," Dad read.

"Must be a search party looking for a lost yacht." Mom nodded toward the helicopter.

Dad hurried to the bow where he stood with his arms at his side. The chopper circled around us, tipping slightly to one side, as if to get a better view. Then it flew around us again, as if to double-check our reply. Perhaps they also verified that nothing looked suspicious onboard, that we weren't held hostage by pirates or something. Then the men nodded and flew off into the distance. We watched silently, until they vanished.

Finally, Dad broke the silence. "Well, I hope they find the boat they're looking for," he said as we returned to finish our interrupted lunch.

Thirty-seven days after leaving Ascension Island, we reached Barbados. Even though this was the longest time we'd spent at sea, we didn't stay long at our first Caribbean island.

"The United States isn't far now." Dad tapped his foot impatiently as he gazed into over the ocean.

Just over two years earlier, we left Australia with plans to circumnavigate the world, with a layover in the United States to visit relatives. Six years before that, Dad left Missouri for Australia. Mom and I stayed with her adopted mom, Nanny, until Dad arranged housing and established himself in Australia. When I was six months old, Mom and I flew to New South Wales to meet him. We hadn't been back to the States since. I wrote letters regularly to Nanny and Grandma, but I didn't remember them. Jolene and Jackie had never met them or any other relatives, since they'd made their entrance into the world in Australia.

We were closing in on our first major goal. The U.S.A.! We stopped at a second island long enough to fill up with freshwater. Then we hustled on, as fast as we could, to the United States.

However, the wind failed. Again. This leg of the journey lasted longer than expected. Far too long. As we sat becalmed, our food supplies slowly dwindled. Our freshwater was getting low, too. Mom still had the supplies to make damper, our Australian pan bread. We had plenty of peanut butter, lots of onions, a few eggs, and many cans of beans.

"What's that?" I pointed to the food Mom served.

"Peanut butter and onion sandwiches," she said with a smile that didn't reach her eyes. She set the plate in front of me.

"Peanut butter and onion?" I picked up the top piece of damper. I wrinkled my nose and shook my head.

Mom said softly, "Cheryl, we don't have many options right now. Be glad you've got something to eat."

I was hungry, but I looked at the sandwich doubtfully. If I didn't it eat it, Mom would save it for later. The next time I asked for something to eat, she'd bring out this same plate of food. Food wasn't thrown away at sea. It was too precious, too hard to come by, so we wasted nothing.

Sighing, I lifted the sandwich and took a bite. The raw, crisp onion was tangy—too tangy, in my opinion—but I was hungry, so I ate it.

"Mmm," Dad said with a sigh, after taking a large bite. "This is good stuff. I could live off these." We didn't have much choice, so it was smart to enjoy the sandwiches. To enjoy them as long as they lasted.

We had to be close to Florida, though we couldn't see it yet. A small bird dropped on our deck one afternoon, but it wasn't a seagull, a pelican, or any other sea bird. Apparently, this little animal had been blown off course, far from his home on land, and wanted a place to rest. He gobbled up the tiny flying fish that regularly landed on our deck, and he showed no sign of wanting to leave the security of our boat.

As we sat becalmed, we befriended our new passenger. "Let's name him. How about George?" Dad suggested.

"Won't he need a passport to get through customs?" Jolene asked. I wasn't sure if she was serious or playing along with Dad's silly suggestion.

Dad cocked his head. With a serious expression on his face but a twinkle in his eye, he seemed to consider her idea. "You're absolutely right," he said. "We don't want any trouble with the law. He'll need proper papers. We'd better help him get his papers in order. Cheryl," he said, turning to me. "Go get some paper."

I scrambled into the cabin and returned with a couple of sheets of notebook paper and some crayons. Dad folded the paper in half, forming a little booklet. Imitating the design of our real passports, he wrote "passport" on the outside. Inside the front cover, he drew a simple picture of a bird.

"What's our bird's full name?" he asked.

Mr. George Bird of Florida soon had a passport. I drew a stamp showing he'd officially visited the *Berenice*. Jolene colored George's picture.

On July 12, 1973, we still sat becalmed, making no headway. It seemed like weeks since we'd made any progress. The adults weren't playful any more. Jolene and I spent much time in our private bedroom, away from the adults who seemed to grow angry at the least thing.

"I think I'll make a cake," Mom announced. She pulled out a bowl and spoon and flipped the pages in her cookbook.

"What are you doing?" Dad looked at her as though she were about to commit murder.

"Making a cake. We have a couple of eggs left. I thought I'd celebrate my own birthday." Mom bit her lip and looked down.

"Oh no, you won't!" Dad ordered. He usually left food decisions to Mom, but a cake would use the last of the flour and eggs. We had one more onion. A few traces of brown paste lined the sides of the peanut butter jar. A couple of cans of beans remained. The freshwater faucet gave only a trickle of water. We were in serious trouble.

A humming noise caught my attention. Slowly, it grew to a rumble. Something was coming closer. Mom and Dad rushed on deck, with Jolene and me following close behind.

In the distance was a large, gray ship. Even its lifeboats were bigger than the *Berenice*. Uniformed men bustled about on her deck. The sea churned around her as she pushed her way toward us. An American flag flew above her. Soon the roar of her engines drowned out all other sounds, and the Coast Guard insignia became clear.

"Need assistance?" a man's voice boomed over a megaphone.

What a relief!

"We're not damaged, but we're low on food and water. We'd appreciate a tow," Dad yelled.

The next thing I knew, we were all aboard the United States Coast Guard ship. My sisters and I were in their huge galley with Mom, having a snack. The huge galley, with several long tables, was larger than our entire boat. After several meals of peanut butter and onion sandwiches, their food tasted wonderful. Dad was allowed to stay on deck to watch over the *Berenice* as she was towed to Port Everglades, near Miami, Florida.

34. A Sudden End

Finally, we were in the United States! We'd made it to Florida!

After the Coast Guard dropped us off, Dad exchanged some money for American cash. Then, he searched for a payphone and called his mother in Missouri. "We're here!"

"When can you get to Missouri?" she asked. "I've arranged a big family reunion. Relatives from all over the country are coming in a few weeks to meet you and your family. People I haven't seen in years. They want to see you and hear about your adventures before you leave."

"As soon as I get the details worked out, we'll fly up there," he told her. "Could you loan me a car when we get there? I want to drive back here and pick up a few things. We won't be able to bring much on an airplane—not enough to keep us for a few months."

He planned to stay in Missouri, visit relatives, rest, and earn some more money. Then we would pick up our voyage where we left off. We'd return to Australia via the Panama Canal and settle down once more. Dad hired a man to watch the *Berenice*, to guard against thieves and vandals, while we were more than a thousand miles away.

We packed a few bags and took a taxi to the airport. In the large airplane, with its comfortable seats and uniformed stewardesses serving snacks, it took only two hours to travel a distance that would have taken weeks or months to sail. At the busy Atlanta airport, we hustled down one hallway and up another, through throngs of people, to catch our connecting flight to Kansas City. Voices all around us had accents like Mom and Dad. At the final airport, in Kansas City, we collected our bags from the spinning carousel and found our way to a Greyhound Bus station. We climbed aboard a bus bound for the small farming community of Jamesport.

The towering buildings, heavy traffic, and crowds of the big city were soon replaced by farms and rolling hills. We passed a yellow sign with a picture of a horse-drawn carriage. Later the bus drove past one of the slow-moving vehicles driven by a farmer wearing a straw hat, a blue cotton shirt, and plain blue pants. The woman beside him looked as though she'd stepped out of a history book, with her white cotton bonnet and plain, long dress.

"Cheryl, wake up." Mom shook me. She picked up sleeping Jackie, while Dad hoisted Jolene over his shoulder.

The bus had stopped in the middle of nowhere, at the side of a two-lane highway, surrounded by fields of corn and soybeans. The bus driver stepped outside, lifted a low door at the bottom of the bus, and pulled out our bags. Mom passed Jackie to me, and I balanced the newly woken toddler on my hip. Mom grabbed two bags, and Dad juggled the other luggage and sleeping Jolene. We trudged along the grass beside the highway, and then turned onto a small dirt side road.

Past a field of plants that were almost as tall as me, we reached a large green lawn, dotted with a few leafy trees. At the top of the hill, the lawn ended at a two-story wooden farmhouse with a porch in front. A swing, with a seat wide enough to hold three people, occupied one end of the porch. A tractor stood to the side of a gravel driveway. Behind the house, a large chicken coop stood on one side, and a big red barn on the other.

The screen door opened, and a tiny auburn-haired woman in a cotton dress ran out, her arms opened wide, toward Dad. A somber-looking man in denim overalls followed her out the door and stood silently on the porch, with his arms folded.

"Mom!" Dad greeted her with a smile, setting the luggage down. "Long time no see."

"Let me look at you," she said, turning to us. "Let me see. You must be Cheryl." She pointed at me. "Do you remember me? Oh, my, what am I saying? Of course, you don't, but I remember you when you were a tiny little thing. I'm your Grandma. And this must be Jolene."

Jolene had woken up and stood rubbing her eyes.

"Why, you look so much like me as a child!" Grandma continued. "And here's baby Jackie and, of course, Carolyn." She gave Mom a quick hug.

"Oh, let us help you with your bags. Come on in. Here's Manuel." Looking at Jolene and then me, she reintroduced him, "That's Grandpa. Come on in." She led us up the porch and held the door open.

Grandpa nodded, grabbed a couple of bags, and carried them inside. He set them down and asked, "Where do you want these?"

"I've prepared the rooms upstairs for them," Grandma said. Then turning to Dad, she added, "It'll be crowded, but it'll do for now."

The house seemed huge compared to the *Berenice*, but then I guess most any house would. A piano downstairs held lots of photos. More hung on the walls nearby. Several were photos of us, but many were of people I didn't recognize. She led us back into a large kitchen, then turned, and opened a door to a narrow set of stairs. We left our bags upstairs and returned downstairs.

"How about some iced tea and a bite to eat?" she asked, as we sat at the kitchen table.

Grandma chatted with Mom and Dad. Grandpa glared and grunted occasionally. When I spoke up, asking the way to the toilet, Grandma's eyes grew large.

From inside the bathroom, I heard her shriek, "Oh, my! Why, Cheryl sounds just like a little foreigner!"

"Well," said Mom, "if you think about it, she is a foreigner. She's lived most of her life outside the States, so of course she speaks differently. She's an Australian child, really. Naturally, she has an Australian accent."

"Humph!" Grandma shook her head as I returned to the room.

Dad borrowed a car and drove to Florida to pick up more of our belongings. He planned to drive nonstop and be back in a few days, but the day we expected him came and went. A few more days passed without any sign of him. Finally, he pulled up in the driveway.

The grim set of his mouth and his deflated look made it clear that something had gone wrong. Seriously wrong.

"While we were gone, the *Berenice* was broken into, despite the guard I hired. Thieves took everything that wasn't nailed down. All the equipment. Things we can't afford to replace."

Mom gasped and plunked into the nearest chair. Silence filled the room.

"What will we do?" Mom finally asked.

"I sold the *Berenice* while there was something left to sell," he said quietly.

Even the little starfish I'd been given for my eighth birthday, months earlier, was gone. Stolen. Dad had packed our few remaining personal possessions and stuffed them into Grandma's car. Our home for two years, the boat he'd worked so hard to build, was gone. His dream was gone.

"Now what?" Mom asked quietly.

"I guess we're stuck here." He shrugged his shoulders. "At least we're with family. We'll stay here until I find a job and figure out what to do next."

And so our voyage around the world ended.

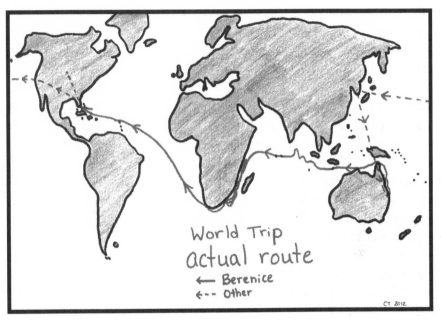

The actual route taken around the world. Solid line shows the path taken by the *Berenice*. The dotted line shows the path taken by other means.

EPILOGUE

We came to Australia when I was six months old. While Dad was at Cleveland Chiropractic College, he learned of an Australian government program that promised free airfare for the entire family and lots of assistance establishing a business for men willing to settle in Australia. Australian wanted trained men, as the country had not yet recovered from the loss of so many men in World War II. Dad saw an opportunity to start his own business, despite the expenses of a family, much sooner than possible in the United States. And Mom? Well, Mom was willing to go along with anything Dad suggested, as long as the family stayed together.

Staying together was the utmost priority to Mom. She bounced around a lot as a child. With an alcoholic dad and a mother who collapsed under the pressure of the situation, she and her siblings were separated and sent to live with relatives. When the situation lasted longer than relatives anticipated, she found herself in foster care. In those days, social workers thought foster children should move often, so they wouldn't grow too used to a temporary home. Eventually, she lived in an orphanage, before she was adopted as a teen. She knew that few homeless teens are lucky enough to find a forever family. She swore to herself that her own family would stick together no matter what. As long as the family stayed together, she went along with almost any idea Dad had. When he was determined to sail the world, she insisted we all come along or the trip wouldn't happen.

On May 30, 1971, we set sail in a 39-foot, ferro-cement ketch, with berths for nine people. My dad, a novice boat-builder, built her himself. At six-and-a-half years old, I was young for second grade by American standards, but I began school in Australia where I began a two-year kindergarten program when I was three. Jolene was five years old, and Jackie was only six days old when our voyage began. Dad intended to sail around the world, ending the journey in Australia, our adopted homeland.

A little more than two years after leaving Hervey Bay, Australia, we arrived in the United States. A month after our arrival, my little brother was born. He was born prematurely, in need of eye surgeries. Doctors predicted he would be a "slow learner," but my mom wasn't convinced. Eventually, he graduated from a state university with majors in the classics (Latin and Greek) and physics, as well as minors in math and history. With a master's degree in physics and published articles in an international physics journal, he's clearly proven them wrong.

Wanderlust seemed to fill Dad's soul as we moved at least once a year. After living in Missouri a few years, in three different towns and more than four different houses, we moved to the Rio Grande Valley in the southernmost tip of Texas, less than a dozen miles north of Mexico.

After a few years in Texas, we finally settled down enough to live in one home for more than three years. In our backyard, Dad built a second yacht. This one wasn't built from scratch or made of cement. Rather, he bought a huge decommissioned steel lifeboat that was designed to hold more than a hundred people. He gutted her, removing everything, until only the steel hull remained. Then Dad rebuilt her, over the course of two years, in his spare time—just as he'd built the first yacht.

Dad had not given up his dream of sailing around the world. He hoped to finish the original journey in this new boat, and he expanded his dream. Instead of sailing through the Panama Canal to Australia, he now planned to sail to Europe first. Then he would cross the Atlantic again, journey through the Panama Canal, and finally return to Australia.

In 1982, almost eleven years after setting out on the *Berenice*, my family left Brownsville, Texas on the next leg of the journey. I was not onboard this time. I stayed behind, living with family friends, to finish my last two months at Donna High School, where I graduated as valedictorian. I went on to the University of Chicago and earned a degree in mathematics four years later. I believe the unorthodox homeschooling methods of my parents and the fabulous foundation I received from Dad's unusual math lessons played a large role in those accomplishments. I learned much more than the multiplication tables that Dad meant to teach, as I watched him convert foreign currency, calculate our position, set new courses, and so on.

On their second yacht, my family quickly encountered trouble. The voyage across the Gulf of Mexico to Florida took much longer than planned. Their yacht ran aground in places where the charts said the water was more than deep enough. The trip that should have taken two weeks stretched into two months. Hurricane season was about to begin. Having endured one cyclone in a small yacht was enough. Dad waited in a safe harbor in Florida for the end of hurricane season. After seven or eight months, they would continue on to Europe. At least, that was the plan, but we know life doesn't always work as planned.

One thing led to another. After a few months, my parents felt settled in South Florida and weren't ready to leave. For the next eight years, they lived on their boat, moored on the St. Lucie River. My siblings eventually graduated from local public high schools and started college. Finally, Mom talked Dad into building the house of her dreams, a yellow house with a porch and a fireplace. They moved off the boat and sold it.

What about Dad's dream of sailing around the world? He sailed more than two-thirds of the way. Many people would say that was good enough. Managing it with three young children onboard, including a newborn, was amazing. Despite tight finances and unforeseen difficulties, he did what few dare to do, and survived with memories of great adventures.

Some might say the story isn't over. Dad is retired now, but he still toys with the idea of setting sail again. His budget doesn't have room for buying a seaworthy boat, but having built two already, that shouldn't be a problem. Convincing Mom to leave her grandchildren would be the difficult part.

However, I'd like to suggest another possibility. I think someone else finished the journey for Dad. Perhaps it didn't end exactly as he had in mind, but dreams rarely turn out just as planned.

Twenty-five years after the *Berenice* embarked from Australia, I flew westward to South Korea. I took a job teaching science at Seoul American High School, a school run by the Department of Defense for the children of American military and embassy personnel. While living and working there, I toured the Korean countryside, explored the streets of Seoul, froze in a Folk Village, camped in the mountains, boated down the Han River, toured a tunnel under the DMZ, and more.

I explored other parts of the world during school holidays. I flew to Hong Kong with several other teachers, shortly before the British returned Hong Kong to the Chinese. I toured the countryside, hiked around the center of the city, strolled through an exotic temple, took a tram to the top of Victoria Peak, shopped, enjoyed high tea in a fancy British hotel, and admired a stretch of water full of Chinese junks. I spent a week chaperoning students in Japan's Tsukuba City for the Junior Science and Humanities Symposium. There I watched traditional martial arts demonstrations, picnicked in a magnificent private garden, toured various science facilities, visited NASDA where Japanese astronauts trained for the International Space Station, sang karaoke, and walked the city.

Then, I saw an advertisement in an army base newspaper offering a special package deal for an off-season trip to Australia over Spring Break. I couldn't resist. From my hotel room high above Sydney, I gazed at the harbor full of sailboats of all sizes, and I sighed. I walked through Hyde Park, taking a detour through a mint museum, to the famous Sydney Opera House. Strolling around the building shaped like a group of sails, I breathed in the clean scent of salty sea air. Sounds of slapping waves, calling sea birds, and chatting Aussies brought back vivid memories. The classic cotton outfits of a group of young children sitting at a café table outside the opera house looked so much like those I'd worn as a child. I toured a zoo full of animals I remembered so well—koalas, wallabies, kookaburras, lorikeets, and more. I watched a sheep-shearing contest. Tea from a billy, and damper cooked in a campfire, reminded me of meals Mom made on our voyage.

After a couple of days, I flew to Cairns, a resort town along the Great Barrier Reef, north of Hervey Bay. Cairns was one of many harbors we visited on our voyage on the *Berenice* so many years earlier. In the evening, I wandered through a flea market where vendors hawked didgeridoos, boomerangs, toy kangaroos and koalas, and other Australian souvenirs. The fresh, salty smell of the sea perfumed the air. Cawing seagulls and slapping rigging on nearby ships played a melody I'd long forgotten. Together with the Australian-accented English of the locals, memories of earlier days flooded my senses.

"G'day, mate," a vendor said, from his stall of colorful sarongs.

"G'day, mate," I replied. Then it hit me. The Australian accent I'd worked so hard to lose, long ago in Missouri when children teased me so much for being different, that accent was back. It returned unbidden, as though it lay hidden all these years, just waiting to reemerge. Even the thoughts in my head held an Aussie twang. I laughed inwardly when some fellow Yanks in our tour group couldn't understand the Aussie English of a local, and I translated for them.

The next morning, I browsed a market on a wharf and picked up copies of my beloved childhood books *Digit Dick on the Great Barrier Reef* and *Snugglepot and Cuddlepie.* My original copies had fallen apart long ago. I inhaled the savory aroma of Vegemite from a food stand. Others in our tour marveled that shops closed by 7 p.m. and shut their doors at least one day a week. They talked about the strange, laid-back, old-fashioned attitudes of Australia, but I reveled in the memories of childhood.

Then an advertisement for white-water rafting caught my eye. I hadn't been on a boat in years. It sounded like great fun, but no one else in our group was interested. I walked on, window-shopping with the group, but the advertisement wouldn't leave me alone. Finally, I decided that even if no one else came along, I had to do it. I marched back and bought a ticket.

Early the next morning, I climbed onto a boat that reminded me of the large inner tube we'd used as a ferry on Egmont Island, though this one was larger with bench seats and oarlocks. Japanese and British tourists filled the boat. The tour guide gave rowing lessons before we set off. The boat's bumping over the rapids, the splashing water, and the roaring as waves hit the rocks, all felt so familiar. When we reached a relatively calm spot in the river, our guide asked if anyone wanted to swim down river. I leapt over. I scraped over a few rocks before meeting the raft downstream, but I laughed as I climbed back on. My spirits felt higher than they had in years.

The next day, several colleagues joined me on the *Falla*, a 65-foot ketch that once hunted precious pearls. We sailed to the Great Barrier Reef and anchored near one of the lacy, colorful reefs I remembered from childhood. Along with most of the other passengers, I dove overboard to snorkel amongst the tropical fish, turtles, and other creatures I once watched from a distance. A gray shark silently meandered past. Groups of tiny colorful fish darted in and out of the coral. Colorless jellyfish pumped along. Plants swayed gently with the water's movement. All were close enough for me to touch.

After our swim, the *Falla* sailed to a small sandbar. A few tourists waited for a dinghy to row them ashore, but I dove into the water and swam to the tiny island that would later disappear with the incoming tide. Emerging from the water, I felt pinpricks all over my skin.

"Sea lice seem to be out today," a crewman commented. I didn't mind. Swimming those waters again was worth a few stings from larval jellyfish.

A few passengers stretched out on the white sand to get some sun and take a brief nap. Some friends searched for shells. Others waded along the water's edge, kicking sand as they watched stingrays scurry. I explored. The sandbar was only a few yards wide, but it was long enough for me to roam without bumping into anyone else.

Alone at the far end of the tiny island, I stood and drank in the view. With the *Falla* behind me, I gazed over the clear blue water, at the animals beneath, and the sky above. Beyond the faint chatter behind me, I heard the creaking of the *Falla*'s rigging and the sounds of the sea. I felt the breeze, the sun on my face, and smelled the clean, fresh saltwater. I was home. I'd come completely around the world and was on a sailboat on the Great Barrier Reef once again. I'd returned to the beginning. I'd circled the world and finished the journey.

ACKNOWLEDGEMENTS

Many thanks to all who helped me tell my story.

My parents gave my siblings and me a most unusual childhood. While they've talked about writing a book about their journeys, they've kept busy with new adventures. When I tackled the job myself, the log my dad kept from the time we left mainland Australia until he quit the journey (temporarily) in Durban, combined with school records, passport and other documents were invaluable in putting my memories in order. My parents' stories and suggestions helped clear up many details and filled in pieces I hadn't understood as a child. Any errors that remain are mine.

My husband helped push me to polish my story further and actually get it published. He put up with many long nights spent at the computer, writing and rewriting. Without his help, this book would never have seen the light of day.

Long before they were born, my children were the motivation for me to write my history. They've listened to it more than once and offered suggestions for improvement in its telling. It is my gift to them and their future children.

My father-in-law generously assisted us as we sought to make this dream a reality. He encouraged us and saw promise in the venture.

Cindy, Barbara, Dabney, and the members of the Wellington Writer's Critique Group offered invaluable assistance in improving the book. Their help is greatly appreciated.

Wendell Lenhart, publisher of the Trenton Republican-Times, generously gave permission to use his newspaper's articles in my book. The Trenton Republican-Times printed many articles on our voyage as it happened.

The Everlasting One Who kept us safe through all these journeys, Who brought me here to tell the tale, deserves the most thanks of all. Without His protection, we would never have survived all the dangers that made it a true adventure.

DISCUSSION QUESTIONS

1. Cheryl's dad, Wally, dreamed of sailing the world alone. Why does he sail with his entire family instead? Should he have stuck with his original dream? Why or why not?

2. Have you ever had to change your plans in order to do something you really wanted to? If so, explain.

3. Wally was inspired to make this journey by a book he'd read as a child. Has any book ever inspired you to do something? If so, explain.

4. Cheryl's mom, Carolyn, spent time in foster care and an orphanage as a child. How did this affect her outlook on family life? Do you agree with her outlook? Why or why not?

5. The family sailed the world with a baby onboard. The nurses in Maryborough thought the journey was too dangerous for a baby. Should adventures be for adults only? Why or why not?

6. Cheryl was anxious to explore an island. Would you want to explore a strange island? Why or why not? What would you hope to find if you did?
   Optional: Draw a picture of an imaginary island that you hope to explore.

7. Pierre-Paul's mother, Marie, did nothing to stop his destructive behavior. What do you think she should have done about his behavior? Why is Cheryl's mom, Carolyn, reluctant to discipline Pierre-Paul, too? Do you agree with Carolyn's final reaction to his misbehavior? Why or why not?

8. The family reads an article explaining that Egmont Island was deserted due to a change in diet that resulted in a disease. Decades later, the author read that the inhabitants of the Chagos Island group, including Egmont, were forcibly evacuated to provide better security for the new military base on Diego Garcia. Which theory do you find most likely?

9. Why did the *Berenice* not stop in eastern Africa even though supplies were very low? Would you stop for supplies if you sailed in that region? Do such problems still exist there today?

10. Why did Cheryl's dad, Wally, suddenly make a trip to Israel? What did the trip accomplish? Why did Jed tell half-truths about himself and his company?

11. The policeman in Lourenco Marques (now called "Maputo") threatens to jail Wally if he doesn't pay for international telephone calls that Jed made. Do you agree with Wally's solution? Why or why not? What would you have done in his place?

12. When Jolene falls in the water in South Africa, a man on the dock does nothing until help is on the way. Why did he freeze? Could he do anything to prevent such a reaction in future emergencies?

13. The family visits a number of islands and harbors during their voyage. Which one would you most like to visit? Why?

14. Why did Dad sell the *Berenice* so suddenly? What other options, if any, might he have had?

15. The children in the story, as in many families of that time, were left to their own devices more often than most American children today. Discuss the benefits and drawbacks to such childhood freedom.

16. Which part of the story did you enjoy most? Explain your answer.

17. Was this voyage around the world successful? Explain your answer.

18. Would you want to sail around the world? Why or why not.

ACTIVITIES TO EXPLORE

1. How can a cement boat float?
   Take a fist-sized lump of clay. Drop it in water. Does it sink or float?
   Experiment with changing its shape to try to change whether it sinks
   or floats.

   A: You should find that a solid lump of clay sinks, but if you carefully
   shape that same lump of clay into the shape of a bowl or a boat's hull,
   it will float. It may take a few tries to make the shape so it contains
   enough air to float, as the entire container (including the air within it)
   must be lighter than the same volume of water.

2. Can you find the places mentioned in the book on your own map or
   globe?
   Find these continents: Australia, Asia, Africa, North America, and
   South America.
   Which continent(s) were left out of the list?

   Find these oceans: Pacific, Indian, and Atlantic.
   Which ocean is largest?

   Find these states: Queensland, Florida, Missouri, and Texas.
   Which of these states is in Australia?

   Find these cities or towns: Maryborough, Hervey Bay, Maputo
   (formerly Lourenco Marques), Durban, Cape Town, Port Everglades,
   Miami, and Trenton (Missouri).

   Find these islands: Thursday Island, Roti, Christmas Island, Cocos
   Islands, Diego Garcia, Egmont Island, St. Helena, Ascension, and
   Barbados.
   Which island would you most like to visit? Why?

Find these countries: Australia, Indonesia, Vietnam, Mozambique, South Africa, the United States, Korea, and Japan.
Which country is the farthest from where you live? Use a map or globe to measure.

A: The other continents are Antarctica and Europe (though some people consider Europe and Asia to be one large continent).
The Pacific is the largest ocean.
Queensland is a state in Australia; the other states mentioned are in the United States.
Other answers will vary.

3. Can you explain seasonal differences?
   The *Berenice* begins her voyage in May in late autumn. Why is May in fall in Australia but in spring in the United States?

   A: Australia and the United States are in different hemispheres. A globe is usually tilted to show that the earth's axis is on a tilt. This tilt affects the angle at which the sun's rays strike the earth. During May, the earth tilts so the sun's rays strike the northern hemisphere more directly and it is late spring there. At the same time, the earth's tilt means that the southern hemisphere receives less direct sunlight and experiences late autumn.

4. In the story, Dad (and later another crewman) sat on the spreader at the top of the mast when approaching land. How does this help him see land sooner than everyone else onboard?
   Activity to help develop understanding: Take a globe, a ruler, and a lump of clay. Set a tiny lump of clay on the globe. Rest one end of the ruler on the top of the clay. Measure the distance from the clay to where the ruler touches the globe. This would be how far a person that height could see.
   Try the exercise again with a much taller lump of clay. How far between the top of the clay and where the ruler touches now?

   A: The earth's surface is curved. Someone raised higher has a longer line of sight and can see farther. (The globe and clay activity should help demonstrate this.) This is why sailors climb a mast to look for land.

5. Cheryl's mom, Carolyn, makes damper, an Australian pan bread, often throughout the trip. Try making it yourself with Carolyn's recipe.

4 cups of flour (up to half can be oats or other whole-grain flour, the rest should be all-purpose wheat flour)
2 teaspoons baking powder
2 cups water
Optional: ½ to 1 teaspoon salt; if you're daring and have access to seawater, try substituting a mixture of seawater and freshwater for the 2 cups water listed above
Cooking oil

Mix all ingredients in a large bowl. Knead well, adding more flour if necessary to keep it from being too sticky. Divide dough in half; shape one-half into a ball and then flatten it into a circle no more than ¾ of an inch thick. Fry the circle of dough in a small amount of oil in a heavy skillet until the bottom is golden brown; turn over and fry until the other side is golden brown. Repeat with the second half of the dough. Makes two loaves. Can tear chunks off to share a loaf. (Alternatively, the dough can be divided into more than two flattened circles, if desired, to make smaller, individual loaves.)

GLOSSARY

Aft: Near or towards the rear end of a ship (synonym: stern; antonym: bow)

Aground: Partly or completely resting on the bottom of a river, ocean, etc.; a boat that runs aground is unable to move and may have hull damage

Anchor: 1. (noun) A device used to hold a boat in place or at least slow it down; 2. (verb) Choose a place for a boat to stay and then secure it there

Anchorage: A place for anchoring a boat

Becalm: To have too little wind to move a sailboat

Belay: To fasten a rope or other object securely

Below: (noun) Inside a cabin that is below the level of the deck

Bilge: An area inside the hull, under the floor, where water collects from rain, leaks, spills, spray, etc.; the storm sewer of a boat

Boom: A horizontal pole, usually attached to a mast, that secures a sail

Bow: The front end of a boat (antonym: stern or aft)

Bulkhead: An inside wall in a boat cabin

Calipers: A tool for measuring distances on maps, with two metal legs held together by an adjustable screw

Capsize: To turn a boat upside down

Channel: The deeper part of a waterway—a route for boats to travel through

Chart: A map with detailed information on currents, water depth, and other valuable sailing information

Circumnavigate: To sail completely around; especially, to sail completely around the world

Cleat: A device, often shaped like a droopy capital letter T, that is used to secure ropes

Cockpit: An area of a boat, usually sunken slightly below deck level with seating and storage areas, which contains the equipment needed for steering

Cooee: A long, shrill call, used as an Australian Aboriginal signal; "within a cooee" is close enough to hear such a signal

Current: A stream of moving water, like a river; within each ocean are many currents

Dinghy: A very small, open row boat; some have a motor

Dock: A raised platform, often made of wood, for boats to tie up to and load or unload passengers or cargo (synonyms: wharf, pier, jetty)

Flare: A device that lights up brightly to signal or give light; a flare gun shoots a flare into the air

Gale: A strong wind

Gale-force: Wind that moves between 32 and 63 miles per hour; stronger than a breeze but not as strong as a storm wind or hurricane

Galley: The kitchen-area of a boat

Genoa: A large, triangle-shaped sail that overlaps the mainsail; sometimes called a "genoa jib"

Harpoon: A spear-like instrument, attached to a rope, that can be thrown or shot

Head: The room on a boat with a toilet and washing facilities

Heel: To tip a boat over, often by a sudden gust of wind or turning a tight curve

Hoist: To raise or lift

Hull: The actual body of a boat; the part that goes into the water

Jetty: A raised platform for boats to tie up to and load or unload passengers and cargo (synonyms: wharf, pier, dock)

Jib: A triangle-shaped sail set in the front of a boat; there are several types of jibs—the genoa jib is the largest

Keel: The bottom part of a hull that resembles a fish's fin; the keel makes a boat more stable, less likely to capsize

Ketch: A sailing vessel with two masts: a larger mainmast in front and a smaller mizzenmast in back

Knot: A measurement of speed; one knot equals about 1.15 statute miles per hour

Line: A rope, usually one used for a specific purpose

Luff: Flap or wave in the wind (said of a sail too loosely tied)

Mainmast: The forward, taller mast on a ketch

Mainsail: The lower sail on the mainmast; the principal sail on a sailboat

Mast: A vertical pole used to hold sails, flags, signals, etc. on a boat

Mizzen: A sail on the smaller mast in the back of a ketch

Mizzenmast: The smaller mast on the back of a ketch

Moor: To secure a boat in place using an anchor, ropes or cables

Navigate: 1. To steer knowledgeably; to figure out where a boat is and how to get it to the desired place; 2. To sail from one place to another

Outback: The large, sparsely-populated area in the center of Australia

Overboard: Over the side; especially, to fall over the side of a boat and into the water below

Pier: A structure built out from the land to the water, used for boats to tie up to, for fisherman to fish from, etc. (synonyms: dock, jetty, wharf)

Port: The left side of a ship when facing the front (antonym: starboard)

Reef: 1. (verb) To shorten a sail by rolling or folding part of it securely; 2. (noun) The rolled or folded section of a sail; 3. (noun) a ridge of rocks, coral or sand

Sand bar: A long, high ridge of sand on the bottom of a river or ocean, created by tides or currents

Sea anchor: A device used to slow down a boat at sea or to keep it pointed into the wind or sea

Sea legs: To be adjusted to the motion of a boat at sea

Seasickness: Sickness caused by the motion of a boat on the waves; someone suffering from seasickness may have an upset stomach, feel dizzy, clammy and miserable, and may even vomit

Sextant: A tool shaped like a triangle with a rounded bottom; a sextant may be used to determine one's location by measuring the angle of the sun (or a star) with the horizon; before modern satellite and GPS technology, most ships used a sextant to navigate

Spinnaker: A large, balloon-shaped sail used in the bow, in front of the mast and the jib

Staysail: A sail attached to a rope or cable that supports the mast, rather than directly to the mast

Starboard: The right side of a ship when facing the front (antonym: port)

Stern: The rear or back end (synonym: aft; antonym: bow)

Tack: To sail in a zigzag pattern in order to sail against the wind

Tiller: A stick or rod used to steer a boat

Trade winds: The nearly constant easterly winds that blow through most of the tropics and subtropics

Wharf: A structure built on the shore and out over the water for boats to tie up to, as well as load or unload passengers or cargo (synonyms: dock, jetty, pier)

Yacht: A type of boat used for private cruising, racing, etc.; a boat bigger than a rowboat or dinghy that is not used for business, fishing, or a navy

REFERENCES

Callen, Wallace, *Log of the Yacht Berenice*. Durban, South Africa: Unpublished log, 1971.

Christmas Island Tourism Association. "Welcome to Christmas Island, a Natural Wonder." Accessed Nov. 22, 2012. http://www.seychelles. travel/en/about_seychelles/index.php

Earthtrust. "Dolphins." Accessed Nov. 27, 2012. http://earthtrust.org/ wlcurric/dolphins.html

Fact Monster. "Sea Snake." Accessed Nov. 20, 2012. http://www. factmonster.com/encyclopedia/science/sea-snake.html

Lenhart, Wendell, ed., "Callens Will Leave for So. Africa In Near Future," *Trenton Republican-Times,* ca. Aug. 1971.

Lenhart, Wendell, ed., "Former Local Resident Plans World Cruise In "Home Built" Yacht," *Trenton Republican-Times,* ca. April 1971.

Lenhart, Wendell, ed., "Former Trenton Couple Finds Plenty of Room in Australia," *Trenton Republican-Times,* Nov. 17, 1969.

Mozambique Happenings. "Maputo Bay and Surrounds." Accessed Nov. 27, 2012. http://www.mozambiquehappenings.co.za/ maputohomepage.htm

National Geographic. "Flying Fish Exocoetidae." Accessed Nov. 29, 2012. http://animals.nationalgeographic.com/animals/fish/flying-fish/

Neufeldt, Victoria, ed. *Webster's New World Dictionary.* NY: Warner Books, 1990.

Schult, Joachim. *The Sailing Dictionary*, second edition. Translated and revised by Barbara Webb. Revised for second edition by Jeremy Howard Williams. Dobbs Ferry, NY: Sheridan House, 1992.

Seychelles Tourism Board. "About Seychelles." Accessed Nov. 26, 2012. http://www.seychelles.travel/en/about_seychelles/index.php

Worldatlas. "British Indian Ocean Territory." Accessed Nov. 25, 2012. http://www.worldatlas.com/webimage/countrys/asia/biot.htm

Suggestions for Further Reading

Rees, Leslie. *Digit Dick on the Great Barrier Reef.* Sydney: Ure Smith, 1969.

Samson, John and Geoff Wellens. *How to Build a Ferro-Cement Boat, 2nd ed.* Ladner, B.C.: Samson Marine Design Publishing, 1968.

Slocum, Joshua. *Sailing Alone Around the World: The First Solo Voyage Around the World.* London: Phoenix Press, 1900 (reprinted 2000).

Cover photo:

The *Berenice* is shown in one of the few surviving photos. Dad is at the tiller, steering. David, a crewman, sits on the rail at the stern, near the dinghy hanging on the back. Mom is visible in the cockpit. Cheryl is the girl, eight years old in this photo, whose blonde head is visible in the main cabin's doorway. The photo was taken by a sailor on a passing yacht, which stopped in mid-ocean to trade their beer for our cake, somewhere off the coast of Africa. 1973.

Newspaper articles from Trenton-Republican Times, 1969-1973, reprinted with permission.